Manji

KULDIP NAYAR (1923–2018) began his career as an Urdu reporter in the 1950s. He moved to English journalism with the United News of India (UNI) which he was instrumental in setting up. He later became editor of the Delhi edition of *The Statesman*, and also had a long association with the *Indian Express*. An outspoken critic of Indira Gandhi, he was arrested during the Emergency years (1975–77). He was also a human rights activist, and a member of India's delegation to the United Nations in 1996. He was appointed high commissioner to the UK in 1990 and nominated to the Rajya Sabha in 1997. His weekly columns and op-eds appeared in over eighty newspapers, including the *Deccan Herald*, *The Daily Star*, *The Sunday Guardian*, and *Dawn*, Pakistan. Nayar authored fifteen books, including *Beyond the Lines: An Autobiography*.

ALSO BY KULDIP NAYAR

On
LEADERS
and ICONS

from JINNAH
to MODI

KULDIP
NAYAR

• Foreword by MARK TULLY •

SPEAKING
TIGER

SPEAKING TIGER PUBLISHING PVT. LTD
4381/4, Ansari Road, Daryaganj
New Delhi 110002

First published in India by Speaking Tiger 2018

Copyright © The Estate of Kuldip Nayar 2018

ISBN: 978-93-88326-54-4
eISBN: 978-93-88326-55-1

10 9 8 7 6 5 4 3 2 1

Typeset in Adobe Garamond Pro by SÜRYA, New Delhi

Contents

Foreword

L al Bahadur Shastri, Nehru's successor as prime minister of India, used to call Kuldip Nayar 'lumboo' because he was so tall. He could also be described as one of the tallest, if not the tallest, of Indian journalists who started their careers around the time when India achieved independence. Kuldip had an advantage over most of his contemporaries in that he had seen the other side of the story too by working at the most senior level of government as a very successful press officer. In these memories, Kuldip relates the history of the first seventy-two years of independent India by describing his experiences of working with or reporting on the leading figures of his time, taking us from Mahatma Gandhi to Narendra Modi.

Kuldip had a remarkable ability to get on with people. He was not one of those journalists who feel it's their business to pick fights, to interview aggressively. On the contrary, he sought to understand the people he was reporting on and learnt of stories before anyone else, getting scoops by the trust he inspired. For instance, although the former Pakistani prime minister, Zulfiqar Ali Bhutto, was renowned for his hatred of India, Kuldip got him to admit that he was responsible for persuading the former Pakistani president, General Ayub Khan, to launch the 1965 war against India. Bhutto told Kuldip he believed Pakistan would win because of the superiority of its armour.

Kuldip's experiences suggest answers to several other questions often asked about India's immediate past. He provides evidence that Nehru definitely wanted his daughter, Indira Gandhi, to succeed him. When the succession race started, Kuldip learnt that Morarji Desai had thrown his hat into the ring. He believes the report he filed on this ruled Morarji out of the race, because other Congress leaders did not approve of Morarji making his bid so soon after Nehru's death. Kuldip is able to confirm that Indira resented the rise of Shastri from the time Nehru fell ill and Shastri started dealing with his files. Shastri's widow told Kuldip she was convinced that her husband had been poisoned because she saw that his body had turned blue. When Kuldip asked Sanjay why elections were called in 1977, Sanjay said he should ask his mother, adding that in his scheme of things there was to be no election for three or four decades. This implies that if Indira had won the 1977 election, Sanjay would have used his influence with his mother to retain the Emergency.

In these memories Kuldip expresses his admiration for the leaders of the Independence movement. He admires their financial rectitude, saying, 'they didn't think of money'. He remembers Sardar Vallabhbhai Patel immediately putting in his papers as home minister after a bomb exploded at one of Gandhi's prayer meetings, accepting responsibility for failing to prevent this. Nehru refused to accept his resignation. Kuldip particularly admires Badshah Khan. The man who had been known as the Frontier Gandhi told him that he was deeply disappointed about Nehru's failure to support the Pashtunistan movement.

Kuldip is less complimentary about the leaders of the next generation. For instance, he points out that in 1984 Congress leaders failed to control the anti-Sikh riots which followed Indira Gandhi's assassination in the states where they were in power, whereas opposition leaders ruling the states of West Bengal and Andhra Pradesh showed it was possible to do so by taking decisive action.

Kuldip had always hoped that the relations between India and Pakistan would normalize. He founded the tradition of Indians and Pakistanis assembling on either side of the Wagah border at midnight on August 14/15, the Independence Days of Pakistan and India respectively, holding candles and calling for friendship between the two countries. But finally he comes to the sad conclusion that there is much truth in Nehru's words about Pakistan: 'Kashmir is only a symptom of a disease and that disease is hatred of India.'

Kuldip's passionate belief in secularism as the principle which should guide Indian democracy shines through these memories. He believes it was Mahatma Gandhi's assassination which ensured that India remained a pluralist nation for more than four decades. However, in the last chapter of his memories he says, under Narenda Modi, the one prime minister he didn't meet face to face, 'a diluted form of Hindutva has spread throughout the country,' and he suggests Modi should 'ask himself whether this scenario is good for the people.' He wonders why human rights activists and civil rights workers like him have failed to prevent this and suggests it might be because they have not joined politics. Obviously a long life battling for the good of India ended with sadness. A great journalist, and a good man, felt his life's missions to protect secularism and befriend Pakistan had failed. But these memories and Kuldip's many other writings will inspire others to battle for the causes dear to his heart.

New Delhi   Mark Tully
November 2018

Preface

Left to me, the title of this book would have been 'Heroes, Neros and Zeroes'.

It is easy to sort out heroes because those who led the national struggle, gave their lives for it, aptly fit into the description. Neros are more difficult to define. The original Nero was the emperor of Rome and legend has it that he clapped his hands and played the fiddle while his capital city lay burning before his feet. All those who were fence sitters when the country was in the midst of the fire of the national movement, can be categorized as Neros. Although their patriotism may be given the benefit of doubt, they were afraid to jump lest they got burned by the flames. Posterity will remember them as calculating patriots.

Thousands of the uneducated and backward led by Mahatma Gandhi, who was at the core of the struggle, are by no criteria classifiable as zeroes. They blindly responded to the call for sacrifice and even died in the process. Their names are recorded nowhere and when they were in the thick of the struggle, they knew that their names would not figure anywhere. Yet they were consumed by such passion that all they wanted was to liberate the country from foreign bondage.

Dr Rajendra Prasad, chairman of the Constitutent Assembly elected to draft the Constitution of India, and a respected leader known for his personal sacrifices, proposed that a voter should have minimal educational qualifications. Jawaharlal Nehru, then the prime minister who was piloting the Constitution Bill, angrily got up from his seat and said that the backward and uneducated were the ones who gave all that they had for the Independence struggle. The educated were the toadies and sided with the British. Today, when the qualifications for the voters are being decided, should we tell them that they do not have the right to decide about the future of the country?

There was such a resounding response to Nehru's plea that Rajendra Prasad withdrew the proposal, thereby including all those, whether educated or uneducated, in the list of voters. The zeroes too qualified, those who had made no contribution but came to enjoy the rights of franchise because they were Indians.

I am privy to several examples of sacrifice. I have heard the recollections of those who were in the corridors of DAV College, Lahore, when Bhagat Singh and his two colleagues, Sukhdev and Rajguru, ran past them to their bicycles and disappeared into the crowd. The new generation may be ignorant of who they were and what they did, but they are the ones who willingly went to the gallows. Mahatma Gandhi, who was leading a non-violent movement against the mighty British Empire, did not approve of their belief in violence. Yet he paid them glowing tributes when Sukhdev wrote him a letter in which he described himself and his comrades as 'those who did not matter'. Gandhi said in a statement that he respected their sacrifice and was conscious of their contribution to the country's Independence struggle. He went on to say that though his own way was different, he did not think that their contribution was any less significant.

The British went ahead and hanged Bhagat Singh and his comrades. This was a few days before the Congress session in Karachi. People wore black bands on their arms and openly criticized Gandhi, so much so that they refused to listen to him when he began his speech. Nehru, popular with the younger generation, intervened and tried to pacify the crowd with the argument that Gandhi's way was different and non-violence was a matter of faith with him. He understood India far better than all of them put together. Probably, he had come to the correct conclusion that if it came to guns, the Indian patriots could not match the resources of their British masters.

Gandhi also believed that even the most cruel had somewhere a soft side which would come to prevail after seeing the sacrifice the volunteers made without demur. It was this same spirit that animated people like Martin Luther King in the US and Nelson Mandela in South Africa against their white oppressors.

I recall my meeting with Mandela when Prime Minister Inder Gujral visited Cape Town in 1997. I asked the South African hero how he survived twenty-one years in jail, including many years in solitary confinement. His response was that the lights in Cape Town city would always impel him to think that one day we would be rolling back the darkness and sit in the brightness of independence. He added that he also always had before him the example of the Mahatma and how he had wrested independence from the unwilling hands of the British. Mandela said he was inspired by how Gandhi never deviated from the path of non-violence.

I participated in the anniversary of the Dandi March, the historic event when people went to the sea and challenged the British by extracting salt from the water that was the monopoly of the state. Hundreds of volunteers suffered the brutal lathi charges without showing any resistance. Sometimes I wonder whether this habit of non-resistance has made us accept blatant, brutal barbarities. My mind goes back to the Quit India Movement of 1942 when Indians faced a famine in which three million are said to have died of starvation. In Calcutta there was the Firpo's restaurant with huge glass panes from which the diners could see the people on the pavements. The poor and emaciated outside Firpo's died of starvation but none of these victims threw as much as a pebble against the gleaming glass windows of the restaurant behind which people dined in luxury. Was this inaction by the starving the result of fear of the police, or the spirit of non-violence which Gandhi had inculcated in them? How different was the West where the French masses stormed the barricades after Marie Antoinette commented, 'If they cannot afford bread, let them eat cake.'

In fact, the British could not understand or appreciate till the end Gandhi's non-violence which was closer to the teachings of the Bible that asks believers to turn the other cheek. Maybe that is the difference between the East and the West. Those in the West who say Indians should be ashamed of allowing their stray cows to die on the streets seem to forget that when it comes to human beings the West is more brutal, callous and unaccommodating.

Visitors from the East who visit cities like London always marvel at the way the local populations of dogs, cats and horses are pampered in every way.

In the East such attitudes are unimaginable. The struggle to eke out a daily living is so demanding that it leaves little time to think of other things. It is not so much a lack of idealism but the nitty-gritty of daily existence that becomes all-important.

Yet it must be conceded that the Mahatma had the

environment where he could succeed. In the West he would not have made much difference. The last British prime minister who presided over colonial India, Clement Attlee, said in his farewell remarks that the effect of Mahatma Gandhi's struggle in the British decision to quit India was minimal. What made them quit, he explained, was the naval uprising in Bombay and its possible knock-on effects. The British, according to him, calculated that they could not possibly take on the navy and then perhaps the army, including one and a half million soldiers who had returned home after World War II. They might turn defiant and would be a potent force that the British could not afford to face at a time when they themselves had limited resources to rebuild their country after the destruction of the war.

One question posed by the new generation is—why did the British not kill the Mahatma when they had hanged so many hundreds of others? Despite Attlee's remark that in their estimation the Mahatma did not count, the British calculation probably was that if they were to eliminate the Mahatma, they might face the kind of revolt with which they could not cope.

Gandhi had become a symbol of the struggle for independence all over the world. That may be the reason why all the countries that subsequently freed themselves from the British looked to Gandhi or India for inspiration.

This book may not have narrated the full story of

struggle and sacrifice, but I have tried to bring before the public those people who not only made a name in history, but also lived up to certain ideals. They were not looking for wealth or fame; they were only consumed by the larger idea of coming out of the darkness of slavery to the light of independence. At a time when everything is being weighed in the same scales of money or success, these men and women from the past touch those heights which are difficult to reach today. If my book gives the reader even some idea of their sacrifice and dedication, I would have redeemed the debt we all owe to those who sacrificed everything for the Independence struggle. I have also talked of some men and women from the world of arts and letters, who illumined the way forward after the battle was won, and some from our neighbouring countries who played pivotal roles in the history and politics of the subcontinent.

I am grateful to Gopal, my assistant and secretary, who typed the manuscript dedicatedly and helped me in making the book possible.

1

Mahatma Gandhi

The first thing I did after migrating to Delhi from my home town, Sialkot, Pakistan, was to visit Birla House. I wanted to see for myself the person who had not only won us freedom but had also given us dignity. We, the brown people, were in no way inferior to the white, the British, who had ruled over us for nearly 150 years.

The Mahatma was pacing up and down in a verandah of Birla House, owned by the industrialist Ghanshyam Das Birla. (His son, K.K. Birla, later went on to establish the English daily, the *Hindustan Times*, from Delhi, now run by his daughter, Shobhana Bhartia).

Birla House was the venue of the Mahatma's daily afternoon prayers. This was where excerpts from all the three holy books, the Gita, the Bible and the Quran, were read before the Ram dhun, *Ishwar, Allah Tere Naam,* was recited.

I 'met' Mahatma Gandhi in the sense that I sat before him on the floor to listen to his lecture. People called it prarthana or prayer. One day a Punjabi Hindu objected to the reading of the Quran because he had seen the ugly side of the religion. The prayer meeting was adjourned. The Mahatma refused to hold any further meetings until the objector withdrew his opposition.

The objector was adamant. It took a week before he could be persuaded to withdraw his objection. The prayer meeting was adjourned every day until he eventually got to his feet and said that he was not opposed to the recitation of the Quran.

The Mahatma employed the same approach many years later when Calcutta was engulfed by the fire of communal frenzy. He asked people to surrender their arms within twenty-four hours. All types of weapons, from a long spear to an air rifle, were given up.

Last to come was a bitter Punjabi Hindu who had migrated from Pakistan. He threw a long knife at the Mahatma's feet and said that his only son aged twelve was killed by Muslims. The Mahatma was sorry to hear his tragic story and advised him to pick up a twelve-year-old Muslim orphan from the crowd and bring him up in the best tradition of Islam, so as to shame the bigoted.

Likewise, in Noakhali, then part of undivided Bengal,

where many Hindus had been killed in retaliation to the massacre of Muslims in Calcutta, Gandhi moved among the angry crowds, accompanied by the then prime minister of Bengal, Hussain Shaheed Suhrawardy, asking what was the need or purpose of killing innocents.

One theme Mahatma Gandhi returned to many a time was Hindu–Muslim unity—this was what he preached all his life. He was a broken man because he could not stop the Partition, although he had threatened that it would happen over his dead body. Ironically, he was to die at the hands of a Hindu fanatic.

I myself have often visited Birla House where Mahatma Gandhi held his last sermon, and gone to the place from where he led his prayer meetings. Today the place is itself eloquent, draped in grief and spiritualism.

I was present on the day, in 1948, when Madan Lal, a fanatic Hindu, exploded a bomb behind the place where Gandhi was sitting. Since the Mahatma did not even look behind, I thought that it must have been a firecracker. Only the following day did I learn from newspapers that it was a bomb meant to kill the Mahatma. The next day Sardar Patel, then the home minister, tendered his resignation because he had failed to protect the Mahatma. Nehru turned it down, saying Gandhi expected 'both of us' to build the new India.

After Madan Lal's failed attempt, it was another fanatical Hindu, Nathuram Godse, who pounded bullets into Gandhi's chest, as he was walking to his daily prayer meeting, on 30 January the same year. He died instantly. I was then working at an Urdu newspaper, *Anjam*, published near Jama Masjid, my first job in the profession. I preferred this to a career as a lawyer, the subject in which I had graduated from Lahore a few months before Partition.

I rushed to Birla House where the security was rudimentary. Cars were not checked. Persons on foot were supposed to produce identity papers to get entry.

The Mahatma's body, swathed in white khadi, was lying on a raised wooden platform. I walked on the path which the Mahatma had traversed from his room only a few hours earlier to the venue of prayer. The grass had been trampled upon and a few drops of blood glistened in the receding light.

I have often gone back to the same hallowed place. It makes you feel terribly emotional, even if only for a few seconds.

Lord Mountbatten, India's first Governor General, arrived when I was part of the human circle around the body. He was in uniform. He saluted the body. I also saw Prime Minister Jawaharlal Nehru standing on a wall, his voice choked with tears as he told the people that Bapu was no more.

Nehru's emotional response was as important as the speech he had delivered earlier on the night of 15 August 1947, when the Indian Parliament held its first ever meeting as a sovereign body. In this speech, in which he described the historic moment as India's 'tryst with destiny', Nehru had said, 'On this day our first thoughts go to the architect of this freedom, the father of our nation, who, embodying the old spirit of India, held aloft the torch of freedom and lighted up the darkness that surrounded us.'

Mahatma Gandhi died barely six months after that stirring speech and I never imagined that any Indian would think of Godse as anything but the assassin of the father of the nation. But I was mistaken. Justice Achru Ram Sehgal, who was on the bench that sentenced the killer to death, told me that some women knitted pullovers for Godse. Some of them apparently even went to the extent of making the depraved suggestion that they would like to spend a night with him in his solitary cell. Nathuram Godse himself justified his action in the letter he wrote before he was hanged, saying he had nothing against the Mahatma, but what he preached went in favour of Muslims.

Rajghat, where Gandhi was cremated, was selected by Nehru. The latter had never imagined that his daughter, Indira Gandhi, would one day be cremated near the same place, just like his grandson, Sanjay Gandhi, known for the excesses committed during the Emergency (1975–77).

With the passage of time Gandhi's creed of non-violence has come to be accepted by the world as the only way for nations to sort out their problems with their neighbours. Gandhi's assassination by a Hindu fanatic has consecrated pluralism in India. Whenever there is tension between Hindus and Muslims, Gandhi's martyrdom is recalled. He still guides us decades later with the help of his thoughts enshrined in the Constitution.

2

Khan Abdul Ghaffar Khan

The Frontier Gandhi

When I met Khan Abdul Ghaffar Khan for the first time more than forty years ago, he jolted me by his remark, 'Kya aap log baniya hotay ho?' (Are you people traders?).

For those not familiar with the politics of South Asia, the word 'baniya' is a derogatory term used by some people, particularly Pakistanis, to run down Indians.

So I was taken aback to hear this remark coming from a man who was revered so much in India. Many years earlier he had been a member of the Congress Working Committee and was offered the party presidency, but he preferred to remain an ordinary party worker. He also visited India in 1969 to participate in the celebrations marking Mahatma Gandhi's hundredth birth anniversary. One year before he died, he was conferred the Bharat Ratna. The prestigious Khan Market in New Delhi is named after him.

Unlike Jinnah who believed nationality was synonymous with religion—hence his two-nation theory about the subcontinent—Badshah Khan, as he was popularly known, firmly believed in a united India spanning the distance of religions. He was close to Mahatma Gandhi and a staunch supporter of his principle of non-violence. The people of his home province in the North-West Frontier—the Pashtuns—are associated with tough talking and even tougher action. But under the influence of Mahatma Gandhi, Badshah Khan shunned violence and adopted the methods of peaceful protest. In 1929, he had founded the Khudai Khidmatgar (Servants of God—also known as the Red Shirts) movement, based on a belief in the power of Gandhi's notion of satyagraha or active non-violence, as captured in an oath. He told its members: 'I am going to give you such a weapon that the police and the army will not be able to stand against it. It is the weapon of the Prophet, but you are not aware of it. That weapon is patience and righteousness. No power on earth can stand against it.' Espousing the Mahatma's principles in his province, Badshah Khan came to be known as the Frontier Gandhi.

Badshah Khan strongly opposed the All-India Muslim

League's demand for the partition of India. When the Indian National Congress accepted the Partition plan without consulting the Khudai Khidmatgar leaders, he told the Congress, 'You have thrown us to the wolves.'

A furious Jinnah contemptuously referred to him as a 'Hindu show boy'. Badshah Khan did not care because he had endeared himself to millions by his participation in the Independence movement. In June 1947, he and other Khudai Khidmatgars declared the Bannu Resolution, demanding that the Pashtuns be given a choice to have an independent state of Pashtunistan, consisting of all Pashtun territories of British India, instead of being made to join Pakistan. The British refused this demand.

After Partition, Badshah Khan pledged allegiance to Pakistan, but demanded autonomy for Pashtunistan as an independent state within Pakistan, integrating the North-West Frontier Province (NWFP). This became Khan's lifelong battle. This Frontier Gandhi and his followers in the Khudai Khidmatgar, suffered at the hands of the British before Independence and at the hands of Pakistan after Independence. He was jailed several times between 1948 and 1954, and again in 1956 for opposing the One Unit programme under which the Pakistan government proposed to merge all states of West Pakistan into a single unit. Khan was in jail or in exile for much of the 1960s and 1970s. His followers conferred upon him the title of Badshah Khan—supreme leader.

An embodiment of sacrifice, he was sitting cross-legged on his charpai when I met him in his one-room hut which had a tin sheet serving as an apology for a roof. All the belongings he had were a few earthen utensils and a change of salwar kameez which hung on a string drawn across the room.

Badshah Khan was then living in Kabul. I arrived by accident in Kabul in 1972, because my original destination was Pakistan where I was scheduled to interview President Bhutto. But the Pakistani authorities said my papers for entry were not ready. They put me on the first available flight out of Pakistan and that happened to be going to Kabul.

I had no Afghan visa but a well-wisher advised me to slip a US$10 bill into my passport and that sufficed to get me an entry into Kabul. Our consul general at the time was Salman Haider, later my deputy in London, when I had my diplomatic stint as India's high commissioner.

It was Haider who suggested it might be professionally useful to meet Badshah Khan. He loaned me a car which took me and brought me back from Badshah Khan's home in a single day.

When I arrived at his hut to pay my homage, I thought here was a man who could have held any office in India. So revered was Badshah Khan that he could have easily become President either before or after Dr Rajendra Prasad. But he had preferred launching a movement for his beloved Pashtunistan. He was another icon for my generation, just like Jawaharlal Nehru, which saw stalwarts like him giving their all for freeing the country from subjugation. In those days the criterion to judge a person was not his bank balance but the sacrifice he made for the country's independence.

Mahatma Gandhi was the hero, the highest on the ladder, but there were others like Jawaharlal Nehru, Sardar Vallabhbhai Patel and Maulana Abul Kalam Azad, who were equally revered. They were not fighting for position or money. What drove them was their faith in India's independence. I imagined that they went through the valley of shadows to reach a brighter mountain peak draped in sunlight.

They are the ones who made modern India and gave the country a Constitution which made the polity democratic and secular, also establishing an independent judiciary and free elections. They, the old guard, commanded love and respect as long as they lived because they had come through the fire of self-sacrifice and suffering.

It was not difficult for me to meet Badshah Khan. He had heard of me and when I sought an interview with him, he agreed to meet me.

On the day I met him in his humble home, the first thing he asked was whether it was true that many Muslims had been killed in Gujarat (in the communal riots of 1970), and how this could happen in the land of the Mahatma. 'But Gujarat is the land of Gandhi,' he said, looking disillusioned and helpless. He remarked that he and all those who had fought for freedom believed that once independence was won and the British left, communal violence would be a thing of the past. He went on to say that when India was fighting for its freedom there was no question of Hindus and Muslims.

As I searched for an appropriate response to his query, he startled me with his contemptuous question about baniyas.

It was an expression of his bitterness against Nehru who, he said, had promised him that when India became free, India would see to it that Pashtunistan also became an independent country. Nehru could not fulfil that promise because it would have meant attacking Pakistan. Badshah Khan never forgave him. 'Are you people baniyas who calculate all the time about the gain and loss in what you do?' he asked. I remained silent.

I would not describe my encounter with Badshah Khan as a formal interview. It was more an informal chat with the Frontier Gandhi asking many questions about India. One of the other questions he asked before I left was whether India would help Pashtunistan win freedom from Pakistan. I told him 'Yes.'

I was proved wrong. We did not help him. So it was a double betrayal. On the other hand, it is to Badshah Khan's lasting credit that before and after Partition his

Khudai Khidmatgars protected many Hindus who lived in Pakistani border cities like Peshawar, Quetta and parts of Waziristan. He was again under house arrest in 1988 in Peshawar when he died. According to his wishes, he was buried at his home in Jalalabad in Afghanistan. Tens of thousands of mourners attended his funeral, marching through the Khyber Pass from Peshawar to Jalalabad. There was heavy fighting at the time as the Soviet–Afghan war was in full swing. Though the procession was marred by two bomb explosions that killed fifteen persons, both sides, namely, the communist army and the mujahideen, declared a ceasefire to allow the Frontier Gandhi's burial.

3

Mohammad Ali Jinnah

I was in my second year of law college in Lahore when Mohammad Ali Jinnah came to address the students. Habib, my Kashmiri classmate, was an active member of the Muslim League, and had arranged the function. Initially, he did not invite us, the non-Muslim students. But when he realized at the eleventh hour that the anticipated audience would not fill even a classroom, he pleaded with us to come to listen to 'our Quaid-e-Azam', the title which Mahatma Gandhi had bestowed on Jinnah. I told Habib that since he had not invited us, we were not planning to attend. Habib was a close friend, so I eventually capitulated and went to listen to Jinnah. The classroom remained partly empty.

This was in 1945, two years before Pakistan was constituted and before the British quit India. Jinnah went over the usual arguments that the Muslims and the Hindus were two separate nations which ate different food, wore different clothes and came from different civilizations. Therefore, the Muslims wanted a separate homeland.

After the lecture, he said he would reply to questions if we had any. I asked him two questions that in retrospect proved to be prophetic. The first was: There was already so much animosity between the Hindus and the Muslims that after the formation of Pakistan on the basis of religion, the two communities would be at each other's throats. In reply he said that we would be the best of friends. Germany and France fought wars for hundreds of years and yet they now had good relations.

My second question was: What would be the reaction of Pakistan if a third country was to attack India? He said that the Pakistani soldiers would fight shoulder to shoulder with their Indian counterparts against any invaders. 'Remember, young man, blood is thicker than water,' Jinnah said.

This was classic Jinnah, asserting one position, only to contradict himself a short time later. His love-hate relationship with India was visible throughout his life. He never forgot that tens of millions of Muslims lived on in India and he felt responsible for the privations they faced.

Years later, when Lal Bahadur Shastri was the home minister and I was serving as his information officer, he confided in me that had the Pakistani troops fought by the side of Indian soldiers and driven out the Dragon during the Indo-China war in 1962, it would have been difficult to say 'no' if Pakistan had asked for Kashmir. Would Jinnah have followed a different course of action from General Ayub Khan, Pakistan's President in 1962? It is difficult to say. If he had, the history of relations between India and Pakistan would have been different, neighbourly and friendly.

Jinnah wanted Pakistan to be a secular state. But he could not succeed in suppressing the religious hotheads. Once Pakistan came to be established, Jinnah's dream of having a Muslim-majority secular country went awry. Jamaat-e-Islami fanatics came to the fore and forced Pakistan to be Islamic.

In his first speech as President of the newly formed nation, Jinnah had said:

'I know there are people who do not quite agree with the division of India and the partition of the Punjab and Bengal. Much has been said against it, but now that it has been accepted, it is the duty of every one of us to loyally abide by it and honourably act according to the agreement which is now final and binding on all. But you must remember, as I have said, that this mighty revolution that has taken place is unprecedented. One can quite understand the feeling that exists between the two communities wherever one community is in majority and the other is in minority. But the question is, whether it was possible or practicable to act otherwise than what has been done. A division had to take place. On both sides, in Hindustan and Pakistan, there are sections of people who may not agree with it, who may not like it; but in my judgement there was no other solution, and I am sure future history will record its verdict in favour of it. And what is more, it will be proved by actual experience as we go on, that that was the only solution of India's constitutional problem. Any idea of a united India could never have worked, and in my judgement it would have led us to terrific disaster. Maybe that view is correct; maybe it is not; that remains to be seen. All the same, in this division it was impossible to avoid the question of minorities being in one Dominion or the other.'

Jinnah's speech could not be broadcast by the Pakistan Radio. Religious elements saw to it that it would be suppressed. Only years later, was it broadcast. There was no adverse reaction.

O

Prior to Partition, Jinnah had joined the Indian National Conference, in 1906. He avoided joining the All-India Muslim League which had been formed that same year. Sarojini Naidu, who was at the forefront of the freedom movement, called him an ambassador of Hindu and Muslim unity.

Jinnah became a member of the Muslim League in 1913, after his rift with Gandhi. He wanted to leave his stamp on the country, which he believed would not be possible as long as Nehru and he were in the same party. He gave in to the Muslim League's demands to join them and lead the party.

By then the demand for territorial autonomy, within India, of the North-West Frontier states, which had a majority of Muslims, had been raised in the shape of Pakistan. Jinnah reportedly fuelled the demand to get maximum concessions for the Muslim minority.

Initially, Jinnah felt that a separate homeland was not the solution. But somewhere along the way, articulating the demands for Pakistan, he became convinced that the two communities were so different in their beliefs, dress and food habits that they constituted two separate peoples, two separate nations.

The British had announced that they would leave India on 6 June 1948. The initial plan was not to divide India. The United Kingdom Cabinet Mission of 1946 had come to India to discuss the transfer of power from the British government to the Indian leadership, with the aim of preserving India's unity and granting it independence. The British wanted to keep India and its army united so as to keep it in their system of 'imperial defence' even after granting it independence.

The Mission was formed at the initiative of Clement

Attlee, the British prime minister. It held talks with the representatives of the Indian National Conference and the Muslim League, to determine a power-sharing arrangement between Hindus and Muslims to prevent a communal dispute. The Congress, under Gandhi and Nehru, wanted a strong central government, with more powers than state governments. The All-India Muslim League, under Jinnah, initially wanted to keep India united but with political safeguards to ensure equal power for Muslims in the legislatures because of the wide belief that the British Raj was simply going to turn into a Hindu Raj once the British departed. However, in the 1940 Lahore session of the Muslim League, Jinnah endorsed Partition via the two-nation theory of a West and East Pakistan, citing recent developments—the 1937 provincial elections, refusal of the Congress to recognize the League as the sole mouthpiece of Muslims in India—as a sign of assured enmity from Hindus, culminating in the Lahore Resolution, also known as the Pakistan Resolution.

After discussions with the Congress and the Muslim League, the Cabinet Mission put forward its plan for the composition of the new government on 16 May 1946. In this plan, the creation of a separate Muslim Pakistan was rejected.

Instead, the plan proposed a united, independent Dominion of India, within which the Muslim-majority provinces would be grouped, with Sindh, Punjab,

Baluchistan and the North-West Frontier Province forming one group, and Bengal and Assam another. The Hindu-majority provinces in central and southern India would form another group. The central government, stationed in Delhi, would be empowered to handle nationwide affairs, such as defence, finance and foreign affairs, and the rest of the powers would belong to the provinces. An interim government at the centre representing all communities would be installed on the basis of parity between the Hindus and Muslims.

Jinnah accepted the offer. But Nehru said that any state—he had Assam in mind—should be allowed to join any group which the British had enunciated. The Congress accepted the proposals related to the Constitutent Assembly. But since it felt that the Muslim League had been given disproportionate representation, it rejected the idea of the interim government. The Congress was against decentralization and advocated a strong centre. Jinnah changed his entire stand and renewed the demand for Pakistan as a separate nation. He felt betrayed by Nehru's statement.

Attlee, who had served in the Burma war, was keen to have the armed forces of the two countries as a united force, under a joint command. Jinnah flatly said 'no'. He had in mind the bitter experience of having accepted the Cabinet Mission plan and then going back on it because of Nehru's stand. Pakistan was an inevitable reality now.

He rejected even Attlee's personal request to keep something common: Jinnah said he did not 'trust them now.'

After preparing the Partition formula, Lord Louis Mountbatten, the last Viceroy of the Raj, requested Mahatama Gandhi for a meeting. Mountbatten told me when I met him, that he felt there was a halo when the Mahatama walked into the room. Gandhi walked out of the meeting when he heard the word 'Partition'. Mountbatten then called Jinnah. 'Your Pakistan is a reality,' Mountbatten said. He once again tried for some kind of link, however weak, between the two countries. Jinnah once again rejected the suggestion. The rest is history.

○

Despite this bitter parting, Jinnah never himself gave up his links with India. He wanted to visit India on a regular basis even after Partition. When Prime Minister Nehru wrote to him and asked what should be done with his two salubrious properties, one in Delhi's prestigious Aurangzeb Road and the other in Bombay's equally prestigious Malabar Hill, Jinnah responded by saying he proposed living in India for periods of time every year. There was no question of confiscating 'enemy' property.

There is one other example that was cited to me by Jinnah's long-serving private secretary, Khurshid Ahmed. This was around 1948 and Khurshid was sitting at the dining table of the Governor General's house in Karachi. Jinnah's sister, Fatima, was also at the table. A young ADC from the Pakistan Navy, whose own family members were apparently killed during the migration, had the courage to pose the question to Jinnah: 'Quaid-e-Azam, was Pakistan a good thing to have?'

The old man did not speak for at least a minute, which Khurshid said actually felt like an hour. Then he said, 'Young man, I do not know. Posterity will judge.'

Jinnah was probably less forgiving to himself in private. Khurshid also recounted, how, a few days after Partition and before he left for Karachi, Jinnah responded when he was told of the many massacres (it is estimated that more than one million were killed on both sides). Jinnah's stunned reaction was summed up in one sentence. 'They are trying to destroy my Pakistan.' He had never anticipated, nor could he believe that killings had taken place on such a vast scale.

Mian Iftikharuddin, a rich man who spent all his life in the Congress but then switched to the Muslim League, tells another story of the deeply affected Jinnah who was flown over the region in a Dakota to see for himself the vast migrations that were underway. According to Iftikharuddin, Jinnah put his head in his hands and whispered, 'What have I done?' The source for this story was Tahira, daughter of Sir Sikandar Hayat Khan, former prime minister of undivided Punjab.

Our own family ordeal was no different from the migration Jinnah viewed from his Dakota. In Sialkot my father summoned the family at our lunch table and announced that he himself was staying back in the newly created state of Pakistan. My elder brother, Rajinder, replied that Muslims would not allow non-Muslims to stay behind. He said he himself had a taste of Pakistan when he was in the medical college at Amritsar. At that time our two communities were evenly divided in the city and the Muslims, who anticipated Amritsar being allocated to Pakistan, would knock on doors to tell non-Muslims to vacate peacefully.

A respectable Muslim family from nearby Jalandhar approached my father, asking him to take their house in exchange for our home in Sialkot. My father repeated to them that there was no question of an exchange, since he was staying back in his home city.

Neither he nor they could anticipate that such a peaceful city as Sialkot would witness the forced migration that followed. Sialkot was a good distance from the Grand Trunk road on which so many migrants travelled between the two countries. When I left Sialkot, the environment was peaceful. But when I hit the GT road, I was shocked to see thousands of people travelling in both directions. That was when I finally understood that there would be no going back.

Never had history seen so many people migrating from one part of the country to the other. So many died and so many were uprooted from their homes in the ethnic cleansing that followed. The gulf between the two communities increased still further after Partition. Muslims in India are still paying the price and the secular Constitution that has been adopted is of little help. Even after seven decades of Partition, the Muslims, roughly 175 million, are generally kept at a distance. Pakistan has done the same with its non-Muslims. They, too, seem to be resigned to their fate.

A report by a commission, headed by the retired Delhi High Court Chief Justice Rajinder Sachar, confirmed that the plight of Muslims in India was worse than that of the Dalits. On the other hand, Pakistan does not have more than three per cent Hindus and Partition on the basis of religion has made it impossible for the two communities to bury the hatchet. Sachar's modest recommendation of affirmative action in favour of Muslims is yet to be implemented.

O

Jinnah's second prophecy that India and Pakistan would be the best of friends like France and Germany has also not come true. New Delhi and Islamabad have fought two wars over Kashmir. They have fought yet another war over the liberation of East Pakistan that helped the East Bengalis to establish their own independent, sovereign country of Bangladesh in 1971.

'I told Jinnah that his moth-eaten Pakistan would not last more than twenty-five years,' reminisced Mountbatten, when I met him at his sprawling mansion, Broadlands, near London on 1 October 1971. This was nine weeks before East Pakistan seceded from West Pakistan.

Seventy-four years old and still with a phenomenal memory, Mountbatten was recapitulating a conversation he had with Jinnah, at the Viceroy's House in New Delhi on 9 April 1947. Mountbatten told him that East Pakistan would become an independent country in twenty-five to thirty years.

'You know, Rajaji (C. Rajagopalachari, Mountbatten's immediate successor as Governor General) wrote me a letter the other day to remind me that my prophecy had come true, and I replied to him that I remembered distinctly what I said,' explained Mountbatten to emphasize that he should not be accused of hindsight.

However, if Mountbatten had indeed told Jinnah this, he must have spoken to very few other people about it. 'Mountbatten's memory probably fails him. I should have known if he had made such a remark,' former Mountbatten press adviser Alan Campbell-Johnson recalled, contradicting the observation in an interview to me at London a few days after my meeting with Mountbatten.

I also checked with Cyril Radcliffe, the lawyer entrusted by the Viceroy to delineate the border between the two

Punjabs and the two Bengals. Radcliffe commented: 'You are the first person to tell me this. I had never heard it before.' Radcliffe never gave me the impression that he regretted what he did. He refused to collect his agreed fee of Rs 40,000, burnt all papers relating to Partition and did not want to be linked with the murders and killings associated with the event. But the fact remains that he drew the lines on the basis of religion both in the east and the west. In his original demarcation plan, Radcliffe allocated Lahore to India. But then he realized that he had not given any significant city to Pakistan. So that was how Lahore became Pakistan's possession.

Jinnah's belief was that Islam would keep West and East Pakistan together. Yet it was wishful thinking that Islam would be sufficient glue to keep together the two wings, which were thousands of miles apart. People living in East Pakistan always felt suppressed and denied of what was their due. They knew that the foreign exchange that Rawalpindi earned was from the sale of jute grown only in the east. Yet it was spent primarily in West Pakistan.

For many years there was no revolt in East Pakistan, although grievances were regularly voiced and protests were held in the streets. But the situation never reached a point of no return until much later. Posterity is a witness that Jinnah himself sowed the seeds of a separate mentality during his first official visit to East Pakistan after the formation of the country. He said in Dhaka that the Bengalis would have to learn Urdu, the country's national language. I think left to themselves they would have probably learnt it in due course, just as the people in South India have accepted Hindi as a link language, along with English. The fact, however remains, that even New Delhi only learned its lessons after burning its fingers. The south was up in flames when Hindi was sought to be imposed without giving them time to learn it. People in the south resented the hurried switchover, some burnt themselves alive on the streets of Chennai.

Pakistan is today facing threats from Sindh and Baluchistan who want their own separate languages. Federal Pakistan has not followed the language formula of India. Maybe they will have to do so at some future date.

O

Jinnah's vision of Pakistan was of a tolerant, progressive and modern state. It is another matter that it has become a purely Islamic one. Jinnah did not live long enough to achieve his vision—he passed away on 11 September 1948, barely a year after the creation of Pakistan. Mahatma Gandhi had fallen to an assassin's bullets a few months earlier. Had both leaders lived longer and led their countries further down the road of independence, Indo-Pak relations might have taken a very different turn for the better.

4

Jawaharlal Nehru

I was in high school when Jawaharlal Nehru, accompanied by Kashmir leader Sheikh Abdullah, came to my home town, Sialkot, in 1935, to address an election rally. I waited for several hours to have a glimpse of him. He was late. Yet people waited patiently to hear Nehru.

At the meeting Nehru admonished the ladies, who started leaving after his arrival. He did not realize that they had no interest in the election. All that they wanted was to have his darshan. Once they had seen him, their desire was fulfilled. Never did I imagine then, that one day I would be his information officer.

On my return from the US, where I had gone to study journalism at the Medill School of Journalism, I had joined the Indian Information Service, and was serving in the home ministry as an information officer. In those days, an officer from the Press Information Bureau (PIB) would be routinely attached to the prime minister. A Catholic officer, Harry D'Phena, was Nehru's information officer in 1963. When D'Phena went on leave I was asked to attend to Nehru till he returned.

Nehru lived in a sprawling two-storey mansion, Teen Murti House, now the Nehru Museum. The bungalow had been the commander-in-chief of the British Indian Army's residence during the Raj. Nehru had moved there after Independence.

I did not know what Nehru expected of me. I was used to the requirements of Home Minister Govind Ballabh Pant, whom I had served as information officer prior to being assigned to Nehru. Pant wanted the information officer to ensure that every word he spoke in public would appear in the press, and to keep him informed about whatever was relevant.

When Chester Bowles, then America's ambassador at New Delhi, commented on India and the government, I rushed to Nehru's residence to report his statement. The gist of Bowles' remarks was that America wanted India to take the initiative to foster good relations with Pakistan. I was breathless when I reached the top of the stairs, more so because I was face to face with a person who was my icon. I began speaking excitedly in English. Nehru was patient. He told me to speak in Hindi and slowly. He listened impassively and made no comment when I came to the end of my speech. But his daughter Indira Gandhi later told me that her father had indeed noted what I had told him.

During my deputation with him, he went to Jaipur. A fleet of cars awaited him at the airport. I was surprised that a separate car had been allotted to the information officer. I did not use it because I sat in the prime minister's car in the front with a security person.

When Vijayalakshmi Pandit, his sister, was in town, she would personally drop him at the airport. She was in the car on that occasion too. Newspapers that morning had carried a report on Nehru's address to the Indian Administrative Service (IAS) probationers. Mrs Pandit expressed her surprise over the appearance of his remarks in the press because it was not the practice. Nehru pointed his finger towards me and said that it was my doing. I had briefed the press on the advice he had given probationers that they should pay special heed to the common man. Unlike Pant, for his part Nehru never said a word about whether he had been reported correctly or exhaustively.

He was busy building a modern India and setting up institutions. The parliamentary system was his idea which the Constitutent Assembly had to approve. I personally think that the presidential system would have worked better for the country because the person who became President would have been directly elected by people from different parts of India and would have enjoyed the security of tenure.

Building a structure from scratch was not an easy task. Yet this is Nehru's contribution. He planted deep the seeds of democracy that have sprouted in the shape of a secular Constitution and a democratic polity.

'One person one vote' was his idea even though more than 80 per cent of people were illiterate. Some Constituent Assembly members wanted a voter to have minimum education qualifications. Nehru opposed the proposal. He said that when they were fighting for independence, the educated were on the British side. Now that the country was independent, how could the uneducated or even the illiterate be denied the right to vote. The Partition on the basis of religion had adversely affected the concept of pluralism. But Nehru said that tolerance was a part of the Indian ethos and it should be left to an individual what religion he or she wanted to pursue. Thus democracy and secularism became the foundations of the Constitution.

Conscious that economically backward states had to be brought at par with the rest, Nehru founded the National Development Council (NDC), a body of state chief ministers, under the Planning Commission which was also his brainchild. This is the apex body which plans India's development schemes and harnesses resources to execute them.

Some governments, like the one headed by Prime Minister Narendra Modi, believing in a free economy, have tried to undo the planning. Now the very Planning Commission has been abolished. Planning may well be connected with the ideology of the Left. Yet the fact remains that there cannot be an effective utilization of resources and the uplifting of backward states without an overall assessment of resources and the plan of how to spend them.

Nehru's vision helped India establish Indian Institutes of Technology (IITs). This helped the country stem the tide of brilliant students going abroad for studies in science and technology. It goes to Nehru's credit that he helped the nation to imbibe the scientific temperament. The fact that India is beginning to be accepted as a leading nation in the field of high technology owes much to Nehru's vision and the nation remains indebted to him for looking ahead.

Nehru's main contribution to the world was the concept of non-alignment. During the Cold War which began after World War II between powers in the Eastern Bloc (the Soviet Union and its satellite states) and powers in the Western Bloc (the United States, its NATO allies and others) Nehru constituted a platform of non-alignment where the nations which did not want to align with either bloc gathered to escape the dictates of both. Leading the Non-Aligned Movement (NAM) were India,

Egypt, Indonesia and Yugoslavia. This non-alignment lost its raison d'étre after the end of the Cold War in 1991, when the Soviet Union was dissolved.

○

Nehru's weakness was his daughter, Indira Gandhi. He may have denied it in public, but in reality he wanted her to succeed him. This was thinking on the lines of Mughal kings and, in my view, Nehru followed that type of thinking though he may never have enunciated it.

His immediate successor, Lal Bahadur Shastri, would often say in those days: 'Unke man main to siraf unki putri hai' (He has only his daughter in view). Once when Nehru fell ill, I told Shastri to get ready to be anointed. This had been Shastri's response.

Indeed, Shastri was right. When it came to a successor to Nehru after his death, her name came to the fore. Morarji Desai was her staunchest opponent. 'That chit of a girl', he remarked while rejecting a consensus name. Congress President K. Kamaraj preferred Shastri. He was considered a key which could fit into any lock. However, Morarji did not withdraw from the field. He was not impressed by the argument that Indira was the daughter of Nehru, the country's icon and therefore suitable for succession.

When I wrote after Nehru's death that Morarji was the first one to throw his hat in the ring, the impact of my exclusive UNI report was devastating. There was public outrage, especially amongst the Congress and its supporters, that Morarji had put forward his candidature even before Nehru's ashes had grown cold, and it destroyed his chances of success. Shastri remained unruffled. He called me to his house to say: 'No more story; the contest for leadership is over.' He meant that the story had swung the pendulum in his favour and that he was as good as elected. Kamaraj personally thanked me for my role in this. I was flabbergasted because I had done a journalist's job, without any motive. The full story is told in a subsequent chapter.

Staunch followers of Nehru tried their best to make Indira Gandhi the next prime minister. But Shastri was preferred to her because he was more widely accepted. Kamaraj subsequently told me that Nehru had indicated his preference for Shastri as his immediate successor when he appointed him as minister without portfolio after all ministers, including Morarji, had given their resignation letters to him under the Kamaraj Plan, which was essentially to oust ministers of the old guard who dared to criticize Nehru after the Chinese defeated us in 1962.

When Kamaraj once discussed the matter of succession with him, Nehru was deliberately vague. He said that the people were the best judge in a democratic polity. Yet he mentioned the names of Shastri and Indira during the discussion.

As a true and loyal soldier, Kamaraj had in mind first Shastri and then Indira as the prime minister. In the election of both, Kamaraj played a key role. Morarji was rebuffed every time because Kamaraj represented mainline Congress opinion and he personally did not want Morarji.

○

There was open criticism of Nehru for having lionized Chou En-lai, the Chinese premiere. Indeed, Nehru had put him on the world stage and helped Communist China to get a seat in the United Nations Security Council. Nehru did admit that he was personally betrayed by Chou En-lai when he attacked India. But his admission of an error of judgement was not weighty enough to assuage the feelings of a defeated nation.

One fallout was that people began to see that Nehru was a god who had failed. He began to be criticized by the Congress leaders themselves. Yet they continued to support him because he was the only leader who, despite the debacle, had no peer. People, by and large, continued to follow him because they had nobody else who was a familiar figure from the days of the freedom struggle. Moreover, Mahatama Gandhi had preferred him as his lieutenant, not Morarji. Yet the impact of China's betrayal was so great that Nehru's health began to decline, and he spent many months in 1963 in his beloved Kashmir, recuperating.

In the January of 1964, Nehru suffered a stroke. This was the time when Indira Gandhi ruled the country in the name of her ailing father. Even the bedridden Nehru was powerful because of the general support he continued to command.

Shastri, as minister without portfolio, began quietly dealing with the files marked to Nehru. Indira did not like this. She would insist on seeing important files herself before sending them to Shastri. Shastri learnt of this but did not protest. On one occasion, in 1963, when I was still Nehru's information officer, I had gone to Teen Murti house and saw Shastri, then out of power, waiting outside Nehru's office for more than an hour. I pointed out to N.K. Sheshan, Nehru's private secretary, that Shastri had been waiting for a long time to meet Nehru. Sheshan told me that he had twice sent a message upstairs to Nehru's bedroom. 'What can I do when she (Indira) is not calling him,' he said, and advised me to keep away from 'their politics.'

In May 1964, Nehru had gone to Dehradun to stay with Vijayalakshmi Pandit who had built a house there. He returned to Delhi on 26 May, apparently refreshed from his brief holiday, and retired to bed as usual at 11.30 p.m., but at around 6.30 a.m., he rose to go to the bathroom. He complained of a pain his back and collapsed. Indira immediately summoned three doctors who had been attending to him since he had suffered the stroke. They tried everything they could to revive him but Nehru never regained consciousness. His death was announced to a stunned nation on the afternoon of 27 May 1964. India was plunged into mourning. The nation was numbed, a sense of insecurity and uncertainty prevailed.

Nehru's ashes were disseminated all over the country, as was his wish. He said he had received love from people all over India and hence his ashes should be dispersed in all corners of the country. His other wish that his daughter Indira should be one of those to succeed him also came true, after the death of Shastri.

I was present at Nehru's funeral, a dot in an ocean of mourners who had gathered on the banks of the Yamuna. A man of the world, a man of the masses, a master of the written and spoken word; innumerable images flashed through my mind as I stood there. I went back to his *Discovery of India* to read: 'Life is a continuous struggle of man against man, of man against his surroundings; a struggle on the physical, intellectual and moral plane out of which new things take shape and fresh ideas are born.'

After the cremation, I rewrote the introduction of the UNI story that I had filed: 'The man who was Jawaharlal Nehru was now a handful of ashes.' For me, he represented all that India was after Independence.

5

Lal Bahadur Shastri

Govind Ballabh Pant was the home minister in Jawaharlal Nehru's government. When he passed away in March 1961, Nehru allotted the portfolio of home to Lal Bahadur Shastri who was then heading the commerce ministry

Shastri retained his old dependable staff and added two more. One was Pant's chauffeur, who drove the car too fast. I was the other. Shastri believed that the vast publicity Pant got was because of me. Indeed Pant would take me along wherever he went, even in an ancient, two-engine Dakota which had a limited number of seats. I was told that Shashtri had said, 'Woh lumboo ko rakho. Pantji ko bahut publicity dilvatha tha.'

I was called 'lumboo' because I am six feet tall and Shastri by contrast was less than five feet in height. When

I walked next to him, we must have made an incongruous sight as I loomed over the prime minister-to-be.

The first challenge which confronted Shastri was when he was sent to Srinagar which was up in arms because the Prophet Mohammad's hair (Muay Mubarak) had been stolen. Soon after Shastri reached Srinagar, a Muslim leader met him and offered to help. His assistance came with a price, some favour in return. I do not know what was the quid pro quo. But the hair was recovered to everybody's relief. Shastri had the hair verified before announcing its recovery. I found him thorough, going over every minor detail. Nehru complimented him in Parliament for having solved the crisis over the hair.

My role in unwittingly helping Shastri to become prime minister is not widely known, so I shall tell it here. Nehru had been cremated the previous day, on 27 May 1964, and Congress MPs were still grieving the loss of their leader when I wrote a story distributed through UNI saying that Morarji Desai had put in a bid for the prime ministership. This was my understanding after talking to various interested individuals and groups alike. I still recall Moraji's son, Kanti, saying, 'You can tell Shastri that the game is over and we have the overwhelming support.'

When my story came out, Congress MPs were disgusted by what they saw as Morarji's crude ambition. By one reckoning at least 100 hitherto undecided MPs switched their support overnight to Shastri. The game was indeed up, but it was Morarji who lost.

Later when I went to apologize to Morarji, saying I had not deliberately tried to sway the election, he did not believe me. When I tried to assure him that Shastri had no hand in my report, he merely said that Shastri had many ways to influence a person.

Morarji never forgave me and suspected for the rest of his life that I had filed that story purely in order to help Shastri. Many years later when the Janata government was formed with Morarji as prime minister, external affairs minister Atal Bihari Vajpayee proposed sending me to Rome as India's ambassador. But time and again Morarji said no. The story repeated itself with the Janata home minister Charan Singh who wanted to appoint me as joint governor for Punjab and Haryana. Once again, so I was told, Morarji stood in the way.

O

Shastri had always been very particular to have with him the Congress leaders from the south. In fact, they had met at the temple town of Tirupati where they chose him as Nehru's successor. Austere and simple, Shastri was their unanimous choice. Other party leaders thought they would be able to manage him. This was their mistake and they realized it, but by then Shastri had consolidated his position.

People consistently underestimated Shastri because of his slight frame and dimunitive stature. It was almost as if he was a man of the masses who had somehow risen to high office. But there was much more to him that was not immediately visible. He was both decisive and firm with qualities of statesmanship that were to be admired. I still remember his observation after the 1962 war with China, when he was home minister, when he told me, 'If Pakistan's forces had fought side by side with us, it would have been difficult to say no if they asked for Kashmir.'

The truth is that he nursed a burning ambition to take over after Nehru. All of us who worked with him could see that he wanted nothing more than to become India's next prime minister. People also never forgot that he served Nehru honestly and loyally.

Immediately after Nehru's death, Morarji's son Kanti was busy collating lists of possible supporters. In a deeply conservative society like India this came across as sacrilegious. In sharp contrast Shastri spent his time and energy helping to supervise Nehru's funeral rites.

O

It must have been around midnight IST when there was a loud banging on the door of my hotel room in Tashkent. It was a Russian lady. 'Your prime minister is dying,' she told me agitatedly.

Russian Prime Minister Kosygin had forced India and Pakistan to come to the negotiating table to formally call an end to the 1965 war between the two countries. One of his aides had jokingly told our side, 'We will feed you kebabs in Tashkent.' That was how we found ourselves in this Russian border city in January 1966.

It so happened that I had had a premonition that Lal Bahadur Shastri would die during the peace talks. Because of my premonition I was not altogether surprised when the knocking started on my door. Inwardly, I was prepared for the worst.

Shastri and General Mohammad Ayub Khan, Pakistan's President, were housed in luxury dachas some fifteen kilometres away from the Tashkent hotel where the rest of us were staying. J.S. Teja, press and culture minister at the Indian embassy in Moscow, hurriedly arranged for us to be driven to Shastri's dacha. Kosygin himself was standing in the verandah when we got there. He looked in my direction and gestured to say Shastri was no more.

I was the first one to enter the prime minister's massive room. Inside a cavernous space and stretched out on a huge bed lay the prime minister's body draped in a dhoti and vest. No telephone or call button was visible. This contradicts what external affairs minister Swaran Singh later told Parliament. Namely, that a call button was available.

Afterwards, one of Shastri's stenos who had accompanied him to Tashkent explained the sequence of events on that fateful night. It seems that Shastri suffered a massive heart attack, but still had the strength to walk to his steno's room to ask, 'Doctor?'

Venkatraman, the steno, told me how he walked Shastri back to his bed while somehow managing to also call his personal physician, Dr R.N. Chugh, who did what he could, including administering an injection straight into his heart. It was too late. A grieving Chugh said, 'Babuji, you did not give me a chance.'

Whether Shastri was poisoned, as some have alleged, is still a matter of debate. What is known is that he was a victim of two earlier heart attacks and on the final night he asked his personal valet, Ram Nath, to get him some milk and then some water. When the prime minister finally succumbed, an overturned thermos was discovered on a table in his dressing room. Shastri had gone to bed slightly agitated because the accompanying Indian media had badgered him with questions about why he had returned the two conquered posts of Haji Pir and Tithwal to Pakistan. These and other issues were weighing heavily on his mind, including his attempt to make telephone contact with his wife, Lalitha, who he affectionately referred to as 'Amma'. But Amma refused to speak to him because she too was upset at his decision to give back these territories to Pakistan.

As we stood around, Swaran Singh turned to me and asked, 'Kuldip, who do you think could be the next prime minister?' I repeated to him what Shastri had himself told me a few months earlier, 'If I die in the next two years, my successor will be Indira Gandhi. If I survive, it will be

Y.B. Chavan (then the defence minister).' Chavan, who was also part of our group that day, commented, 'Kuldip, make sure you write this down somewhere.'

A few hours later we were on our way to the airport and all the citizens of Tashkent seemed to be out on the streets with outstretched arms trying to make physical contact with any member of the Indian contingent. Shastri's body, along with his accompanying ministers, was flown by a special Soviet aircraft that flew over Pakistani air space to get to Delhi. We Indian journalists were in a separate Air India aircraft that now could overfly Pakistan. Earlier on our way into Tashkent strained relations with Pakistan meant we had to travel via Iran.

Shastri's plane landed in Delhi about an hour before us. I went straight to his residence. He was yet to be cremated. When I went to convey my condolences to Mrs Shastri, she admonished me, 'Where were you? Can't you see he has been poisoned, his whole body is blue.' What could I say?

The politics about the cremation started immediately. Mrs Gandhi wanted Shastri cremated far away from Delhi, in his home town of Allahabad. She did not think it fitting that he should be cremated in Raj Ghat, on the banks of the Yamuna in Delhi, as had been done in the case of her father.

This was when Lalitha Shastri stood her ground and warned that she would undertake a fast unto death if her husband was not cremated in the Raj Ghat complex where the last rites were performed for both Mahatma Gandhi and Jawaharlal Nehru. Mrs Gandhi had no choice but to give in and Shastri was cremated at Raj Ghat. His samadhi, Vijay Ghat, stands a little distance away from Nehru's memorial, Shanti Vana. This was one of Mrs Shastri's two threats. It so happened that Mrs Gandhi opposed inscribing on the samadhi the slogan, 'Jai Jawan, Jai Kisan', a slogan originally coined by Shastri himself. Once again Mrs Shastri threatened self-immolation if the slogan was not inscribed. Once again Mrs Gandhi backed down.

Nehru and his daughter were not on the same page as far as Shastri was concerned. Indira probably did not like the fact that he did not belong to any elite family. This was made clear when she went round to his residence after his death and after her election as the head of the Congress parliamentary party.

Shastri's house in the heart of Lutyens' Delhi could easily have been converted into the new prime minister's residence. It was up to Indira to decide. 'Middle class living' was her scornful remark after she toured the premises. The place was left to the Shastri family, which converted part of it into his memorial.

The government spends a large amount on the maintenance of Indira Gandhi's house where she was assassinated. But there is hardly any allocation for the upkeep of Shastri's place. The Congress establishment perpetuates Nehru's legacy. After any major event the posters it puts up highlight the lives of Nehru, Indira Gandhi and Rajiv Gandhi. Shastri does not figure. Probably the thinking is that after Mahatma Gandhi, the Nehru family—Indira Gandhi and Rajiv Gandhi—sold better than the person who had no Gandhi surname. Very few knew that Feroze Gandhi, Indira Gandhi's husband, belonged to the Gandhi caste within the Parsi community, he was not an upper caste Brahmin. Whatever the reason, the name sold well. Indira Gandhi and Rajiv Gandhi were cremated following the Hindu tradition. There was no reference to the Parsi connections of Feroze.

○

People still remember Shastri as the man who defeated Pakistan in the 1965 war. At one stage as the Indian army suffered some reverses in Kashmir, Indian generals went to Shastri and explained the situation could be brought under control but only if India opened a second front in Punjab. When Shastri asked what was the problem, they responded, 'We will have to cross the international border.' Shastri gave his assent immediately.

As Lieutenant General Harbaksh Singh commented afterwards, 'This was such an important decision and yet the prime minister took no time in telling the generals to do the needful. Years later I personally asked Mrs Gandhi what her father would have done. She claimed that he too would have listened to the generals, in effect belittling Shastri's achievement.'

During Shastri's last month, I was in the process of moving to my new job as the head of UNI. When the prime minister died at his Tashkent dacha, I was fortunate enough to be able to use the telephone to call my UNI colleagues in Delhi and instruct them to send a flash, saying 'Shastri dead.'

The man I spoke to at UNI headquarters, Sunder Dhingra, did not believe me at first. He was still in the process of editing the prime minister's banquet speech and it took a bit of shouting down the telephone line to get him to understand what had happened and take the necessary action.

For me Shastri's death was a personal loss. For Shastri's family I was always 'lumboo' and they trusted me because they had seen the devotion with which I served Govind Ballabh Pant.

To this day I remember his austere living, including his simple clothes and frugal needs. Once when we were returning from a trip to the Qutab Minar in south Delhi, we had to stop by a railway crossing because the gate was shut to allow the train to pass. As we waited he saw in the distance a man selling sugar cane juice. Without a second thought he turned to me and said 'Nayar sahib, let's have some juice.' So we got out of the car, walked up to the juice seller and drank a glass each. Despite my protests, he insisted on paying.

Once Shastri was no more, there was no question of my remaining in government service. In any case I was in the process of moving to UNI and the new prime minister, whomsoever it was, would have found it difficult to persuade me to stay on.

This was certainly the case with Mrs Gandhi. She wanted her own people around her and I was not part of that inner clique, nor did I aspire to be.

6

Indira Gandhi

I met Indira Gandhi for the first time when she was chairperson of the Citizens' Committee which Nehru had set up to boost the morale of the people in the wake of defeat at the hands of China in 1962. Nehru had put her in the chair.

Lal Bahadur Shastri was the home minister and a member of the committee, which came under the home ministry. As his information officer, I had to attend the meetings and brief the press.

Earlier, in 1959, Congress president U.N. Dhebar, knowing Nehru's mind, had proposed Indira's name as his successor when he decided to step down as party president. Govind Ballabh Pant was then the home minister. He was not aware that Dhebar would propose the name of Indira Gandhi to please Nehru. Pant could not support this proposal. He was careful not to oppose Nehru's daughter directly but argued that her frail health would come in the way of the extensive travels that the Congress president was required to undertake. Raising his voice, Nehru told Pant that 'she is healthier than both of us' and could put in longer hours of work.

There was no further discussion. Indira Gandhi was unanimously elected party president, and thereby crossed the first major hurdle to the prime ministership.

I found Indira Gandhi to be an informal person and struck up a friendship with her when I saw that she had no airs and graces about being the prime minister's daughter. We became so friendly that when she had her hair cut short, she asked me how she looked. I told her, 'Indira, you were beautiful before and now you look even more beautiful.'

Yet she hardly spent time before the mirror. She was too engrossed in politics and she was conscious of the fact that her father was grooming her to be his successor. And she expected Nehru's loyalist, Lal Bahadur Shastri, to pave the way.

Shastri did propose two names: Jayaprakash Narayan and Indira Gandhi, in that order. Shastri's priority was to avoid an election which he feared might split the party. Significantly, the nation on the whole too did not want the party to break up because the Congress, despite its defects, gave the country a sense of unity. The Congress could claim that it had a follower even in a remote village. Indeed, it was the party that had led the freedom movement. For the people, it was the leadership of Mahatma Gandhi, Jawaharlal Nehru and Sardar Patel that was important. Indira Gandhi was hailed because she was Nehru's daughter, not because Kamaraj, who had taken over as Congress president in 1964, considered her the best person to counter Morarji Desai.

Eventually, Kamaraj announced the name of Shastri as Nehru's successor. Being head of the party, Kamaraj was asked to find a consensus candidate because that was what the party MPs wanted. He chose Shastri over Indira, because at the time, he was more widely accepted in both the north and the south.

'That chit of a girl' was the remark Morarji Desai made when Shastri had proposed Indira Gandhi's name as Nehru's successor. The dislike was mutual. Indira Gandhi, too, had a low opinion of Morarji. When she did come to occupy the prime minister's chair, after the death of Shastri, and had to accommodate Morarji in the cabinet, she did not give him the key ministry of finance, lest she should convey the impression that she had to placate her rival.

On one occasion, I met her to tell her not to humiliate Morarji. How long had I known him, she asked me. Even before I could reply she said that one word aptly described him: 'humbug.'

O

When Indira Gandhi became prime minister for the first time in 1966, the authoritarian streak that later came to characterize her was not so obvious. She was quiet and kept to herself. Socialist MP Ram Manohar Lohia went so far as to describe her as the 'goongi goodiya' (dumb doll). This did not prevent Lohia and Mrs Gandhi from enjoying close personal relations. Years later when Lohia was jailed for some political misbehaviour, the prime minister sent him a crate of mangoes to assure him that she harboured no personal ill feeling towards him.

In those early years the goongi goodiya was not used to public speaking. Her participation in the Lok Sabha was an embarrassment to the party because she couldn't speak coherently. Party propagandists liked to boast that their leader went to Oxford. The truth of the matter is that she lasted no more than six months in that august university. By the time she came to the forefront of Indian politics as the Congress leader, she was far from being a fluent orator in either English or Hindi.

Her progress in improving her oratorial skills in both languages helped her consolidate her position in the party, so much so that she managed to sideline party elders like S.K. Patil, Atulya Ghosh and even Kamaraj, who had made her a cabinet minister. Once after they had been well and truly relegated to the shadows, I bumped into Kamaraj and asked him how he explained Indira Gandhi's style of government. Kamaraj looked at me and hit his forehead with the palm of his hand, to express his helplessness. Indira concentrated power in herself and brooked no criticism.

She gave that message to newspapers. The *Indian Express* was an exception and did not dance to her tune. In retaliation she stopped all government and public sector advertisements to the *Express*. But it was commendable that the paper's owner, Ramnath Goenka, left it to us on the staff to run the paper. We did not relent in denouncing her. Years later she made us the first target when she imposed the Emergency. The board of the *Indian Express* was changed and the *Hindustan Times* owner, K.K. Birla, was appointed its chairman by Sanjay Gandhi, the then extra-constitutional authority. Birla obeyed him both in letter and spirit.

So successful were Indira Gandhi's tactics that people across the country started to describe her as 'the only man in the cabinet'. She survived every national crisis, including severe food, water and power shortages. Her greatest moment of glory came in the 1971 war when she managed to split the two wings of Pakistan, helping the emergence of Bangladesh. She was by now so popular that even political opponents like Atal Bihari Vajpayee took to describing her as the all-powerful Goddess Durga.

In her success also came the seeds of failure. Elections had taken place before the 1971 war, but in a startling, retrospective judgement four years later in 1975, the

Allahabad High Court ruled that Indira Gandhi was personally guilty of electoral malpractice and barred her from holding any elected office for another six years.

After the Allahabad judgement, Indira had thought of stepping down. I believe that if she had done so and had gone back to the people for a verdict on her electoral offence, offering her apologies, she would have got re-elected. However, two persons dissuaded her from doing so. One was her principal adviser and son, Sanjay Gandhi, who completely ruled out her resignation. The other was Siddhartha Shankar Ray, then the West Bengal chief minister, who advised her to impose an Emergency. She reportedly told him that India was already under an Emergency following the Bangladesh war. He said what he meant was an internal Emergency which would enable her to suspend fundamental rights and allow her to rule as she wished.

Instead of appealing against the judgement, Indira Gandhi imposed a state of Emergency, including strict censorship and detaining her most feared political adversaries. On a personal note, I too, was detained because of my critical writing. For three months, I lived in Tihar Jail until the Delhi High Court ordered my release.

Meanwhile Indira became ever more dictatorial and paranoid. She gave full leeway to her younger and more favoured son, Sanjay, who became the real power behind the throne. A dropout from the Doon School and an apprentice motor mechanic with Rolls Royce in England, Sanjay had no educational qualifications but was keen to enter politics. It was he who launched Maruti cars and it was Sanjay again who decided on compulsory sterilization for any family that had more than two children. No questions were asked of the rich. It was mostly poor men on the streets of North and South India who were dragged into vasectomy clinics and forced to experience the horrors of sterilization.

Two years after imposing the Emergency, Indira Gandhi felt the need for political legitimacy. She did not like being called a dictator and was very encouraged when the Intelligence Bureau (IB) told her she would win any election hands down. In fact, the opposite happened. The Congress lost heavily, particularly in North India, and Indira Gandhi was forced to resign.

I was given an appointment to come to the prime minister's house. She was outside in the garden. When she saw me she walked towards me. But I looked at her and said, 'Today I have come to see Sanjay.'

Her political heir apparent was standing some distance away, under a tree in the garden. I got an inkling of Sanjay Gandhi's thinking during our conversation. I was writing my book, *The Judgement*. Kamal Nath, his friend and a director on the Indian Express Board, had arranged the meeting. My first question to him was: How did he think he would get away with it? He said that if elections had not been held they would have been running the government. Then, why did you hold them? I asked. 'You should address that question to my mother,' he said. 'In my scheme of things, there were to be no elections for three to four decades.'

How would you have ruled? I inquired. 'There are enough bureaucrats who are of my thinking,' he said. 'In any case, there was hardly any instance of disobedience during the Emergency. Fear had done the job. I had persons like Bansi Lal (then defence minister), who would have seen to the compliance of what we had in mind.' He had not changed although the apparatus he had built lay in a shambles after the Emergency.

He had always been his mother's favourite. About her other, older son, Rajiv, she used to say, 'He doesn't know anything about politics.'

It must have been a very bleak time for Indira Gandhi and both sons when the Congress lost the 1977 elections. Rajiv and his Italian-born wife, Sonia, were so disgusted by all that had happened in the run up to 1977 that they were considering packing their bags to go and settle in Italy.

At that point neither Indira Gandhi nor Sanjay and their followers in the Congress could have predicted they would come back with an overwhelming majority in 1980. But the coalition government headed by Morarji Desai made a mess of things with endless squabbles between Morarji and Charan Singh, then the home minister.

What the public wanted was a government that stood for stability and decisiveness and Indira Gandhi with all her faults was judged to be a better option.

To be fair, Indira Gandhi did display some humility when she returned to power. When I met her at her residence for an interview, she was surrounded by a group of close advisers. Turning to me, she said, 'Yes, I made a mistake.' Following that afternoon, we never met again except for one meeting where we exchanged cursory greetings.

Sanjay was even more remote. He was now an MP in his own right and had acquired political legitimacy. The big question in everyone's mind was what he and his wife Maneka would do. The public was frightened of them, as the speculation was that they could get away with anything, including committing atrocities.

As it turned out, there was no need to be concerned. One late afternoon Sanjay drove to the Safdarjung Flying Club from where he and an instructor took an aircraft up for a spin. The plane crashed a few minutes later and both Sanjay and his instructor were instantly killed.

Indira Gandhi went back to the site of the crash and there was speculation at the time that she was searching for the key to a safety deposit box. Pictures taken at the time showed a devastated mother and there was admiration for the composure and dignity that she displayed.

From then onwards it was downhill all the way for

Indira Gandhi. The Congress started to lose its lustre, especially in the party's stronghold of Punjab. It so happened that the country's President at the time was a Sikh, Giani Zail Singh, Indira Gandhi's own nominee. Later the two fell out because Indira's new heir apparent, Rajiv, suspected that Zail Singh was quietly assisting Sikh terrorists.

In a bid to control Zail Singh and his friends among the Akali Party, the Congress came up with a solution in the shape of a Sikh preacher called Sant Jarnail Singh Bhindranwale. No one knew that Bhindranwale would in turn become a Frankenstein, using his power of oratory and deep knowledge of Sikhism to challenge the Congress.

As his popularity soared, it became clear that he wanted to be recognized as a power in his own right, something that Indira Gandhi was afraid to give him. He said that he did not want Khalistan (an independent Sikh state), but if it was handed to him he would not say no. From the safety of his headquarters inside the Golden Temple, he issued challenge after challenge to the government in New Delhi. He even went so far as to publicly abuse Indira Gandhi.

The prime minister picked up the gauntlet and ordered the army to storm the Golden Temple, the Sikh Vatican, sacred to the Sikh community. When the army encountered stiff resistance from the heart of the Golden Temple, a decision had to be made about whether it would be appropriate to use tanks. Indira Gandhi was woken up in the middle of the night to ask if the security forces could go ahead with all guns blazing. She gave her approval, but in the process alienated the entire Sikh community.

To this day even moderate Sikhs argue that other methods could have been used, such as cutting off all water and electricity supplies. Why, they ask, did their beloved Golden Temple have to suffer such desecration ?

Among the alienated Sikhs were the prime minister's two hitherto ultra loyal Sikh bodyguards deployed at the entrance to the prime minister's residence. Soon after the Golden Temple operation, on 31 October 1984, Indira Gandhi had a television interview scheduled with renowned film producer and actor Peter Ustinov. At 9.20 a.m. that morning, as she walked across the lawns connecting her residence, 1 Safdarjung Road, with her office, 1 Akbar Road, where the interview was to be held, the two bodyguards, Beant Singh and Satwant Singh, opened fire, pumping their bullets into Indira Gandhi. Beant Singh shot her with his pistol. As she fell to the ground, Satwant Singh fired at her with his Sten gun. Her secretary, R.K. Dhawan, who was accompanying her, told me that he was at a loss to believe what he was seeing. Beant Singh said in Punjabi, 'We have done what we had to do. Now you can do what you have to do.' Both guards dropped their weapons and surrendered to the police. Indira was rushed to the All India Medical Institute (AIIMS) where she breathed her last.

Only days earlier the Intelligence Bureau had warned that the two men posed a security risk and should be replaced. She disregarded their warnings, saying, 'I have full faith in them.'

The first anti-Sikh riots were reported from Calcutta outside Writers' Building. Many analysts later concluded that Rajiv Gandhi was saved because he happened to be in West Bengal when his mother was killed. Jyoti Basu, the chief minister of West Bengal, who was attending a trade union conference in Tamil Nadu, rushed back to his state and deployed paramilitary and police forces to nip any violence in the bud.

The same was true of Andhra Pradesh where N.T. Rama Rao took a strong position that not one Sikh should be harmed in his state and security forces were deployed to protect the life and property of the Sikhs.

Unfortunately, this was not true of the Hindi heartland ruled by Congress (I) chief ministers. Violence erupted in New Delhi around 4.30 p.m. from outside the All India Institute of Medical Sciences as soon as news of Indira Gandhi's death broke out.

A few buses were stopped, Sikhs pulled out and beaten up, their turbans were removed and set on fire. That was the beginning.

From 31 October to 3 November, the trend continued,

building into a massacre. Sikhs were killed in the most brutal manner. Their necks were ringed with tyres filled with petrol or kerosene oil and then they were set on fire. Sikh business establishments, homes, gurdwaras, schools, colleges were set on fire and finally individual killings built into massacres in Trilokpuri, Sultanpur and Mangolpuri. After Delhi, Bihar saw the worst of the communal carnage—Bokaro, Patna, Dhanbad, Ranchi, Jamshedpur, Bhagalpur, Jhumritalaya and Daulatgang. Rajasthan, Haryana, Uttar Pradesh and Madhya Pradesh were all badly impacted, replicating the killing patterns with striking similarity.

No effort was made to contain violence in Congress (I)-ruled states until Mrs Gandhi was cremated on 3 November 1984. Until the cremation, Doordarshan allowed a free run of slogans: khoon ka badla khoon se lenge (blood for blood). Poisonous rumours were spread to whip up a frenzy against the Sikh community.

In four days over 3,000 men, children and women were massacred. In Delhi alone, the death toll according to official figures was 2,733.

The People's Union for Civil Liberties (PUCL) and People's Union for Democratic Rights (PUDR) visited the affected areas and came up with a report: Who are the Guilty? They named Congress (I) leaders who led the violence. They came up with the following conclusions: The violence began with the floating of a set of rumours on the evening of 31 October. The rumours were three: First, Sikhs were distributing sweets and lighting lamps to celebrate Mrs Gandhi's death; the second rumour was that trainloads of hundreds of Hindu dead bodies had arrived at Old Delhi railway station from Punjab. Third, water was poisoned by the Sikhs.

This raised a hue and cry and the public called upon the government to set up an inquiry commission. Rather than concede to the demand, Rajiv Gandhi tried to resist the pressure and in a public speech at India Gate said: 'When a big tree falls the earth is bound to shake.' He said an inquiry commission would reopen wounds. As pressure continued, the Marwah Commission of Inquiry was instituted to identify guilty police officials in the carnage of 1984.

However, the anti-Sikh violence became a major emotive issue when Rajiv Gandhi initiated the Punjab peace process. An inquiry was a precondition for any such initiative. Rajiv Gandhi agreed and suddenly the Marwah Commission which had already completed its work was wound up and a new Misra Commission of Inquiry was instituted to go into the Delhi violence. It should have covered the entire Hindi heartland wherever there was anti-Sikh violence, but only a few other areas were looked into.

In all there were seven committees set up under an executive order, and three others established after parliamentary resolutions but justice was never delivered.

7

Zulfikar Ali Bhutto

There was more to Zulfikar Ali Bhutto than all the books on him say. He was brilliant, audacious and adventurous and all too conscious of it. This made him arrogant. He could not accept the number two position. He preferred the secession of East Pakistan to a secondary position in a united Pakistan. When Sheikh Mujibur Rahman, the undisputed leader of East Pakistan, swept the polls with his Awami League in Pakistan's first democratic election in 1970, he should have become the prime minister of the country, because he had a majority in the National Assembly. But this was not acceptable to Bhutto because he wanted the top position for himself.

With the help of the army, which was overwhelmingly from West Pakistan, Bhutto established his superiority. He had Mujib and his associates like Kamal Hossain arrested.

Not only that, the army headed first by General Yahya Khan and then by General Tikka Khan committed untold brutalities. Senior army officers used to contemptuously refer to the East Pakistani Muslim masses as 'converts'.

The army deliberately massacred the Bengalis, who it did not like in the first instance. The demand for independence was inevitable. Even then Bhutto did not relent in stopping the indiscriminate killing. That was when the people of East Pakistan, the place where the Muslim League was originally founded, decided to liberate themselves. The rest is too well known. In 1971, Bangladesh was created, with Mujib as its first prime minister.

○

A naval officer clicked his heels and asked me to follow him. I was waiting in a large room to meet Zulfikar Ali Bhutto, Pakistan's President after East Pakistan had liberated itself from distant Rawalpindi and its oppressive military. This was in 1972. As soon as the Bangladesh war had ended, I sent a request for an interview with Bhutto. I had to send my request through the Swiss embassy because India and Pakistan had cut off diplomatic relations with each other. Once my interview request was accepted and I had the official stamp of approval, the Pakistan government's public relations department laid out the red carpet. It is strange that both Indians and Pakistanis should negotiate mutual invitations via a third country but suspect the invited guest from next door.

Without doubt, Bhutto was in full control of what remained of Pakistan. And he was conscious of this. An Italian correspondent, who met him before me, told me that the problem with him was that he was obsessed with himself.

The Italian correspondent also told me that Bhutto seemed to believe that Indira Gandhi would fall in love with him and would sign on any dotted lines. But he found her tough and uncompromising on the return of territory and the 93,000 Pakistani prisoners of war. This was what Pakistan had lost in the 1971 war against India.

When Bhutto met Indira Gandhi at Shimla in 1972 and requested her to return the territory and prisoners unilaterally, initially he drew a blank. The talks between the two leaders began on 28 June and ended on 2 July 1972. Indira Gandhi wondered why Pakistan had brought in the UN Declaration during the talks. She said all matters between India and Pakistan should be bilaterally resolved without any third-party intervention, and that the subcontinent should refuse to be a pawn in the game of the great powers. Bhutto said that he, too, was not 'going to rush around the chanceries of the world, because even after twenty-five years of doing so the world has not helped.' He assured her that the reference to the UN was never meant either to involve the international organization or any third party.

Bhutto told Indira Gandhi that he had to get the POWs released and assured her that he would demobilize them. On Bangladesh, he gave an undertaking that Pakistan's recognition would be formalized when he met Mujib 'by the end of the month' (July). Indira told him that India had no hesitation in releasing the prisoners but that Bangladesh's concurrence was necessary as they had surrendered to a joint command of the Mukti Bahini and the Indian army.

Bhutto's officials told their Indian counterparts that if he returned empty-handed his position in Pakistan would be greatly weakened. A few non-officials went further and warned India that the failure of the Shimla Summit would mean the beginning of Bhutto's downfall and the return of the army. Still this did not make Indira Gandhi relent. Both sides were so entrenched in their positions that it was thought that the best way out was a joint communiqué to break the news of failure as gently as possible. They put out a statement which read:

'Both Mrs Gandhi and Bhutto discussed all major issues affecting the relations between the two countries. They also specifically talked about Jammu and Kashmir. They expressed the hope that a mutually agreed settlement of all outstanding issues would be possible and that the process of reconciliation initiated in the first meeting of the Heads of the Government would continue.'

The talks failed and Bhutto sent back his luggage. At the farewell meeting, he once again asked her to accede to at least some of Pakistan's demands. By then P.N. Haksar, the prime minister's secretary, had intervened and had convinced Indira Gandhi that even the bit of democracy that Pakistan continued to enjoy would end if Bhutto was not accommodated to some extent. India decided to accommodate Pakistan on the question of the territory occupied during the war. Besides being a gesture, it would convince Bhutto of India's sincerity in seeking a durable peace, a status which D.P. Dhar, who was looking after Bangladesh and Pakistan, had discussed with his Pakistani counterpart, Aziz Ahmed, in Murree.

The reason for returning the territory was because New Delhi did not have to seek Dhaka's concurrence to do so. The Indian army was also finding it difficult to remain in the desert territory which it knew it would eventually have to vacate. New Delhi's stand in international forums was that after a conflict, the victor should never be allowed to retain the fruits of aggression.

In exchange for territory, India wanted to see whether Pakistan would agree to joint inspection teams to ensure that the war machinery in both countries was kept within reasonable proportions, and adjustments in the international border after mutual consultation.

Bhutto was vehemently opposed to both proposals. When he met Mrs Gandhi for a farewell call on 3 July, he said that he would be willing to sign an agreement provided these two proposals were dropped.

India had included the two proposals only as a bargaining counter and did not mind deleting them, but was determined to convert the new ceasefire line into a stable international border. New Delhi had for some time been wanting the UN observers on the ceasefire line to leave because their presence was tantamount to interference by a third party in the affairs of the subcontinent. A new ceasefire line, agreed to by India and Pakistan, would make their role redundant, and that was exactly what New Delhi declared after concluding the agreement with Pakistan.

Bhutto agreed to respect the 'line of control resulting from the ceasefire of 17 December 1971', but added after this sentence in his own hand in the draft agreement, 'without prejudice to the recognized position of either side'. India did not object.

The agreement was signed at 12.40 a.m. on 3 July 1972, after almost everyone had assumed that the summit had failed. So late and unexpected was the development that no typewriter was at hand to prepare a corrected copy of the agreement, nor was the Pakistan government's seal available, having been packed in a box and sent by road to Chandigarh with the other heavy baggage which could not be transported by helicopter from Shimla. As the Pakistan seal could not be affixed on the document, India, too, did not affix its own.

P.N. Haksar later told me that there was an oral agreement according to which Bhutto accepted the ceasefire line as an international border, meaning thereby that Pakistan would retain the territory it held in Kashmir, called Azad Kashmir, and India the rest of the Valley, Jammu and Ladakh. The oral agreement has been denied by Pakistan's leaders, its foreign office, and others.

Every time I have asked even people at the top they have categorically denied its existence. New Delhi swears that Bhutto gave his word and Haksar had confirmed this.

○

Bhutto remained the President of Pakistan for some time following the liberation of East Pakistan. When I met him for my interview in 1972, I reminded him about his remark that Pakistan was prepared to fight a thousand-year war against India. He said it was a slip of the tongue. Yet his bias against Indians was palpable. He did not deny that he had sent infiltrators to Kashmir. His reasoning was that he honestly believed that the Kashmiris would rise against India once they knew that Pakistan was willing to back them.

This was probably true. But Bhutto's timing was wrong. The insurgency began in full force many years later. And it continues in one shape or the other till now. Pakistan's support of militant groups is a proven fact. But the determination by New Delhi to retain Kashmir at any cost has not got diluted either.

When I met Bhutto, I asked him whether the 1965 war was his doing, as Ayub Khan had alleged. Bhutto did not deny it and assumed responsibility for the war. He gave me a long explanation, which I recorded on tape:

'There was a time when militarily, in terms of the big push, in terms of armour, we were superior to India because of the military assistance we were getting. That was the position up to 1965. Now, the Kashmir dispute was not being resolved, and its resolution was also essential for the settlement of our disputes and as it was not being resolved peacefully and as we had this military advantage, we were getting blamed for it. So it would, as a patriotic prudence, be better to say, all right, let us finish this problem and come to terms, come to a settlement ... I thought that with this edge that we had we could have morally justified it. Also, because India was committed to self-determination and it was not being resolved, and we had this situation. But now this position does not exist. I know better than anyone else that it does not exist and that it will not exist in the future also.'

Bhutto assured me that he would never repeat what he had done and that he had 'learnt from history'. That may have been one reason why Nawaz Sharif told Inder Gujral (both were prime ministers at that time) that you could not give us Kashmir, nor could we take it from you.

I saw Bhutto's clout at Tashkent in 1966. Prime

Minister Lal Bahadur Shastri and General Mohammad Ayub Khan, Pakistan's martial law administrator, were discussing how to normalize relations between India and Pakistan after the 1965 war. Bhutto, as Pakistan's foreign minister, was against giving any assurance on avoiding the use of force in settling disputes between the two countries. However, Shastri wanted Ayub to give in writing that any dispute between the two countries would not be settled through force. Ayub was inclined to give such an assurance. But Bhutto considered it a surrender. He walked out of the meeting and warned Ayub that he (Bhutto) would tell the nation that Pakistan had been sold out at Tashkent.

Ayub was afraid that Bhutto would make this into such a big issue that the letter and spirit of the agreement would be lost, regardless of the actual contents. Ayub had brought with him a draft agreement for Shastri's signature, but it did not say anything specific about renunciation of violence. It is another matter that Shastri made Ayub write in hand, 'without resorting to arms'. Bhutto was, of course, a witness to this, and promptly denounced the agreement. He went back to Pakistan to agitate against the pact. It provided grist to Bhutto's propaganda to oust Ayub. Yahya Khan, then the army chief, believed only in force. He even ordered the killing of Sheikh Mujibur Rahman, the hero of Bangladesh's liberation during the war. Bhutto intervened in the nick of time and had Mujib jailed instead.

When Bangladesh became independent, Bhutto tried his best to have some links, however loose, with this country which till 1971 been a part of Pakistan. But Mujib did not agree. He had become embittered after discovering the atrocities the Pakistan army had committed and had lost all trust in Bhutto. Bhutto had not realized the depth of Bangladeshi hurt.

Bhutto was brilliant and he wanted people to recognize that. At our meeting in 1972, he told me, 'You have met the Sheikh (Mujib) and, of course, Indira Gandhi, your prime minister. Don't you think I deserve to be the prime minister of the subcontinent (which, by then, had been divided into India, Pakistan and Bangaldesh)?' I fumbled for words and did not know what to say. Without waiting for my reply, he said: 'If merit were to be the criterion, I deserve to be the prime minister.' I told myself that it all depended on what you considered merit.

Bhutto always wanted to be at the centre of the stage or, for that matter, power. The rest of his life was an alibi to grab it. East Pakistan would not have seceded if Bhutto had not pushed it to the point where it wanted to liberate itself. Bhutto preferred the break up of Pakistan to Mujib's prime ministership.

During my interview with him, Bhutto told me that his biggest regret was that he failed to win back Mujib, not realizing that he was himself to blame for Pakistan's break up.

His other regret was appointing General Zia-ul-Haq as the army chief. In later years, Pakistan's chief executive, Pervez Musharraf, said that Nawaz Sharif must repent for making him army chief. This only shows how scared the two prime ministers were of the military establishment that they looked for such officers to head the army as would not retard the political process. That both of them had to pay the price for reposing trust in the wrong person does not mean that the effort to cut the army to size was wrong. It only means that the military establishment in Pakistan is so strong that it tolerates civilian rule up to a point, not beyond. Both Bhutto and Sharif committed the mistake of 'going beyond'.

For Kashmir, Bhutto had in mind a Trieste-like solution. Under an agreement signed between Italy and Yugoslavia in October 1954, the Free Territory of Trieste (a disputed land since World War II) was divided between the two countries along the existing demarcation line, with minor changes.

Bhutto felt India and Pakistan could work out a similar arrangement for Kashmir. This proposal was mooted between Indira Gandhi and Bhutto at Shimla, but the latter said he could not sell it to his country after the loss of East Pakistan.

○

Despite civil disorder, the People's Party of Pakistan (PPP), the party which Bhutto had founded in 1967, won the parliamentary elections in 1977 by a wide margin. However, the opposition alleged widespread vote rigging and violence escalated across the country. On 5 July the same year, Bhutto was deposed by his appointed army chief, General Zia-ul-Haq, in a military coup and incarcerated in the central jail in Rawalpindi, where he faced a trial in the Supreme Court of Pakistan for authorizing the murder of a political opponent, Ahmed Raza Khan Kasuri.

When I visited Pakistan at the end of March 1979, Bhutto had been given the death sentence. Soon after my arrival, I interviewed Zia and asked him about Bhutto's mercy petition. 'I believe you are under a lot of pressure from foreign countries to commute Bhutto's death sentence,' I said. Zia vehemently denied any pressure, either from Washington or from Riyadh. He said there was a process for the disposal of a mercy petition which he had already initiated. The cursory manner in which he spoke about the mercy petition reflected his contempt for Bhutto. I inferred that Zia was determined to hang him. I asked him about the procedure. He said it was up to him to decide about the petition. He had only to ring Lahore, where the crime had been committed, to complete the formality. He did not elaborate on the kind of information he was seeking but the confidence he exuded led me to believe that he had already made up his mind to hang Bhutto and now all that was left was the legal formality.

I narrated the entire interview to Yahya Bakhtiyar, who had been my senior in Law College, Lahore, and expressed my fears. Bakhtiyar conveyed what I had said to Bhutto. He told me that Bhutto's reaction was entirely different. He was convinced that his death sentence would be commuted as a result of the pressure from outside. 'Kuldip got it wrong,' Bhutto said.

I returned to Delhi the day after my meeting with Zia. Within a couple of days of my return, on 4 April 1979, I heard that Bhutto had been hanged at the central jail in Rawalpindi. Zia took only the BBC correspondent Mark Tully into confidence and told him about the execution. People in India reacted strongly against the hanging. There were demonstrations in Delhi and elsewhere to condemn Zia who was called a 'murderer'. Morarji Desai, who was then prime minister, merely said that it was an internal matter of Pakistan. Pakistanis were undoubtedly unhappy over Bhutto's execution but were afraid to protest in public. I was disappointed over this response. Here were the people who Bhutto told me would come on to the streets if ever the military took over the country, but they did not dare to utter a word against Zia.

8

Sheikh Mujibur Rahman

If the founder of Bangladesh was alive to day, I wonder if he would acknowledge the debt he owes Pakistan and Zulfikar Ali Bhutto in particular.

Sheikh Mujibur Rahman was destined for the firing squad on the orders of Pakistan's military dictator at the time, General Yahya Khan, who was determined to finish off this 'enemy' of Pakistan. He had issued orders for Mujib to be shot before sundown.

Why this did not happen was because the civilian prime minister, Bhutto, stepped in to argue that Mujib was the undisputed leader of the then East Pakistan.

Before Mujib came under the detention of the Pakistani military, Indian forces were making inroads by sending their sister forces in the Border Security Force (BSF) to assist Mujib's Mukti Bahini in shaking off Pakistan.

Earlier in 1971, Mujib's Awami League had swept the polls in East Pakistan, getting more seats in the country's National Assembly than Bhutto's Pakistan People's Party (PPP). It was natural that Mujib would take over because of his majority. But neither the military, nor the PPP, were prepared for this.

General Mohammad Ayub, the outgoing military dictator and chief martial law administrator, used to make fun of the East Pakistanis. He repeatedly characterized them as 'mere converts' and not fit to hold political power. Similarly, when the forces of West Pakistan were engaged in suppressing the people of East Pakistan, the same argument was used for killing vast numbers 'because they are only converts.'

Enraged East Pakistanis were united in their hatred of the people from the west, a mix of Punjabis, Pathans, Baluchis and Sindhis. Many from these communities had taken up residence in East Pakistan and were numbered among its administrators, shopkeepers and the soldiers stationed in the east.

Actually, the differences had been simmering since March 1948 when Jinnah made his first and last trip to Dacca (Dhaka). It was during that fateful trip that he announced that Urdu would be the official language of both wings of the country. This was unacceptable to the Bengalis, who are so proud of their language and culture.

Protests broke out from time to time, but for the

next twenty-three years the East Pakistanis learned to live in sullen silence. They were not prepared to take on the risk of any major confrontation. This only took place when Mujib and the Awami League won the universal endorsement of their supporters, paving the way to shake off West Pakistan's control.

I must have met Mujib at least four or five times before, during and after the liberation of East Pakistan. Even before, but not on the record, he used to praise Indira Gandhi as the friend of Bengalis. I first interviewed him at Dhan Mandi, a crowded business street of Dhaka, when he was dressed in a loose kurta pyjama. I was offered tea and sandesh during the hour-long interview. He also arranged for me to be given extra sandesh to carry home to Delhi.

On the second occasion his supporters had started referring to him as 'Bangla bandhu' (friend of Bengal). For my part, I addressed him as 'Mujib sahib'. He did not embrace me, but on the other hand he was always extremely warm and affectionate, asking where I was staying and whether I was comfortable.

Soon after the liberation I had yet another candid interview with him when I asked if it was true that he had promised to work towards a 'Commonwealth of East and West Pakistan.' When I put the question to him, Mujib laughed and said Bhutto was telling lies. 'It was Bhutto who made this Commonwealth suggestion,' Mujib stated. 'I simply laughed it off.'

He further elaborated how in that 'Commonwealth' meeting with Bhutto, 'I told him to let me go to Delhi to thank Indira Gandhi after which I will consider your proposal.'

A disappointed Bhutto now realized the game was up. His uppermost thought was how he could save face with what remained of his country. Finding Mujib resolute, he told him, 'I would request you to go to Delhi but not directly. If you are determined to go to Delhi, why not go first via London.' For Bhutto the idea of Mujib going straight to the Indian capital to meet Mrs Gandhi would not have gone down well with the average man on the street in Pakistan.

Right up to the point of departure in December 1971, Mujib did not know which clothes he should pack, warm clothes for London, or lighter clothes for Delhi. This was a dilemma shared with his soon-to-be law minister and later foreign minister, Kamal Hossain, who claimed that probably only the pilot of their PIA aircraft had been properly briefed on where their first stop would be.

It so happened that their first stop was London from where Mujib telephoned Mrs Gandhi to thank her. She responded by inviting him to stop over in Delhi on his way back home.

Ironically, Mujib's enthusiasm for Mrs Gandhi and India was shared by only a few in Bangladesh. I had a taste of it when I visited the Press Club in Dhaka, close to the Sonargaon hotel. When I got there, a crowd of local journalists were vocal in their criticism of India for grabbing huge quantities of their favourite 'hilsa' fish. In my innocence I had taken the risk of asking these Bangladeshi colleagues where I could sample the famed smoked hilsa. They replied, 'If you are all that keen, go to the Calcutta Press Club.' Their sardonic tone reflected their anti-India feeling even in this apparently flippant remark.

When I met Mujib on that same trip, I expressed my chagrin at the anti-India feeling I encountered everywhere. He said the press men I had met were pro-Pakistanis who continued to enjoy a regular stipend from Rawalpindi.

'A Bengali never forgets a debt. If you give him a glass of water, he would remember it,' he said in an allusion to the help received from India. 'Your forces have lost five or six thousand people, how can we forget.'

Mujib remained the undisputed leader of his country. Once I asked him why he had such little security. 'There is no one in Bangladesh who would kill me,' he responded.

Many people have asked me, if he was so popular, why was he killed so soon after liberation, in August 1975. It was not just Mujib himself who was killed. His wife, younger brother, daughters-in-law and other close members of the immediate family were all gunned down. The only ones who escaped because they were abroad were his daughter Sheikh Hasina and another daughter who was in Germany.

Mujib's killers were by no means fundamentalists. They were power-hungry army officers. The chief of the army, General Shafiullah, and the defence intelligence head, Air Vice Marshal Aminul Khan, are said to have been aware of the plot. But General Shafiullah wanted to keep all options open. He told the plotters he would get involved more openly if they were successful. At least one of the plotters, a major, was known to be a heavy drinker. This came to light after he was posted as first secretary at the Bangladesh embassy in Cairo.

To this day most Bangladeshis remember Mujib with affection. He was a fatherly figure, not given to drinking or womanizing. Nor was he as boastful as Bhutto who once asked me, 'Now that you have met all three, who do you think is the greatest in the subcontinent between Mrs Gandhi, Sheikh Mujib and myself?' Mujib would never have demeaned himself by asking such a question.

Dhaka was only a dot on a map for me, when I was growing up in Sialkot, thousands of kilometres away. That East Bengal would one day be a separate, sovereign country, Bangladesh, was beyond my conjecture. All our attention—and agitation—was focused on how to oust the British rulers from the Indian subcontinent.

Even the demand for a separate Muslim homeland was nowhere in the picture at that time. Hindus and Muslims lived together and communal riots erupted rarely. No one had even the faintest idea that the Muslims would have a separate country, not only one but two, Pakistan and Bangladesh.

I am a witness to events leading to Partition, the creation of Pakistan and then Pakistan splitting into two countries, Pakistan and Bangladesh. Why and how did the Muslims who parted company with the Hindus on the basis of religion, separate from their co-religionist Muslims is a question which baffles me even if it is conceded that one set of people cannot rule another set of people.

I was impressed by the freedom of thought and movement in East Pakistan, even when they were ruled from Rawalpindi. I went to Dhaka soon after the guns fell silent. Dhaka airport was in chaos, piles of luggage lay all over. The hurriedly set up immigration counter had a long queue of people waiting. I wondered if the country, with practically no resources, would survive as an independent nation. Then I heard shouts of 'Jai Bangla', people proudly returning to their Sonar Bangla.

They looked like people returning to the Promised Land. I saw signs of strain and poverty, but pride was writ on every face as if each seemed to say: 'We have done it.'

They were not conscious of what was required to build the country. And there was a naïve belief that Mujib would solve their problems. Had there been the same passion in their hearts in the midst of the revolt against West

Pakistan, the job of liberation would have been easier. As it happens after every freedom struggle, a better way of life is expected from the day the guns falls silent.

To some extent the people's frustration was understandable. They had experienced exploitation for a long time. A liberation struggle always exacts a heavy price. And it takes time for all to enjoy the same standard of living. On the other hand, they had the pro-Pakistan elements among them who were still strong. Bureaucrats were the most vocal, comparing their emoluments with what they were getting when they were part of the Pakistani bureaucracy. There was some nostalgia and newspapers still displayed prominently the happenings in West Pakistan, though they had fought a fierce war and thousands of people died, leaving behind helpless widows and orphaned children.

Newspapers carried the details of incidents where the Indian army had 'looted' houses and carried away rugs and other costly things. True, a few such incidents had taken place but the impression created was as if the Indian army was 'an occupation force' which had indulged in looting and plundering in the same way as the Nazis did during World War II. There was hardly any mention of the many thousands of jawans and officers who had given their lives while fighting by the side of the Mukti Bahini, the popular force that wrested East Pakistan from the hands of oppressive West Pakistan.

One last question remains about what happened to the five army officers who killed Mujib. Retribution was exacted by one of Mujib's surviving daughters, Hasina. She became prime minister of Bangladesh in 2009, and has held that office ever since. She set up an independent tribunal to try the men and the bench found them guilty of murder, sentencing them all to death. No doubt the judiciary was seen as the arbiter of their fate. This way Hasina can claim she had no personal hand in deciding what should become of them. But many amongst her critics have their doubts.

9

Sheikh Abdullah

The Emergency was an endless tunnel. Indira Gandhi had imposed it in 1975 to avoid her unseating from the Lok Sabha for a poll offence. She had lost her appeal in the Allahabad High Court and prevailed upon a compliant President Fakhruddin Ali Ahmed to declare a state of Emergency which allowed her to rule by decree.

Overnight, fundamental rights were suspended, the press was gagged and nearly 100,000 people were detained without trial. I was one of them. I was then employed by the *Indian Express* and had frequently criticized Indira in my opinion pieces. So it did not come as a surprise when I, too, got the midnight knock and was put into a van that drove me to Tihar Jail.

In jail I would often discuss with my fellow detainees,

who in the country could influence Mrs Gandhi to end this hated Emergency. Who would bell the cat?

All of us eventually agreed that Sheikh Mohammad Abdullah, then the chief minister of Kashmir, was the right person with both the stature and popularity to tell her to hold elections. The self-styled 'Sher-e-Kashmir' (Lion of Kashmir) was the founding leader of the Jammu and Kashmir National Conference, and the second prime minister of princely Jammu and Kashmir at the time of Independence. He had played a central role in the politics of the state and was known to be close to Indira and earlier, her father Jawaharlal Nehru.

Another option was to explore legal channels. But Raj Narain, the man who had successfully challenged her election in the first place, was not sure whether the full bench of the Supreme Court would ever uphold the judgement against her, much less the high court.

After three months in Tihar Jail, I was released under a habeas corpus petition filed by my wife and all my fellow detainees urged me to go straight to Srinagar to meet the Sheikh.

My flight to Srinagar reached around noon and I immediately sought an interview with him. Apart from being a journalist, I had struck up an easy personal relationship with him when he was detained at a bungalow opposite the *Indian Express* office.

The Sheikh came to my Srinagar hotel that very

afternoon and hugged me with the remark, 'Tum bhi Haji ho gaye' (you, too, have become a pilgrim). He was referring to my detention.

I told him what we expected him to do. He said: 'You do not know her. She is quite capable of arresting me.' He left it at that. I was confused and disappointed. Faces of my cellmates came before me again and again.

Shamin Ahmad Shamin, my friend, who was a Lok Sabha member from Srinagar, had warned me at the airport that Sher Babbar (his personal term of affection for Abdullah) had become too timid to join issue with Mrs Gandhi. We were at a loss what to do.

Shamin suggested that both of us, who each enjoyed the Sheikh's confidence, would issue on his behalf a statement which he would not be able to disown.

The statement we issued demanded the lifting of the Emergency. We were sure that the Sheikh would not be able to disown the statement lest he damage his personal reputation. In that statement, we said that the Emergency should be lifted because it had served its purpose. We had to be careful in what we said. We did not want to be too blatant in criticism lest the Sheikh should deny the statement. Nor did we want to water down the demand for lifting the Emergency.

Shamin went a step further. He, being a Lok Sabha member, raised the matter in Parliament and used the opportunity to condemn Mrs Gandhi vehemently, much to the embarrassment of the ruling Congress. The Sheikh never mentioned the statement even when Shamin and I met him though he must have known we were behind it. Shamin and I were happy that we had projected the Sheikh's real feelings, although he himself did not want to express it then.

His son Farooq Abdullah was distant from politics at that time. I heard him speak at a function at the Aligarh Muslim University. He was so fundamentalist in his approach that I complained to Sheikh Abdullah. The Sheikh asked me to convey this directly to Farooq. But I did not know him so well at that time and did not pursue the matter further. Farooq has again pitched a different line in an Urdu magazine, appearing from Srinagar. In this much later article, he argued that if Sheikh Sahib had been alive he would have been overwhelmed to know that the Kashmiris had picked up the gun to fight for their rights.

I do not claim to know Sheikh Sahib better than his son. But I can vouch for the Sheikh's opposition to violence. He was conscious of the fact that the state had more guns than an individual or a political party could muster and it would be foolhardy to confront the government with weapons.

I feel sometimes that Farooq Abdullah has not yet fully understood the nub of the Kashmir problem. It is Kashmiriat, a secular approach against the communal one. The Sheikh supported Maharaja Hari Singh's accession to India in October 1947, because of the country's secular credentials. The Kashmiriat, the Sheikh would often say, was akin to Sufism, pluralistic in concept and content. When he preferred India he did so because he saw it following a system which was secular and democratic. For that reason, he rejected Pakistan, a theocratic state.

Before India was partitioned, he sent his close associate, Sadiq Sahib, who subsequently became the state chief minister, to Islamabad to get the feel of Pakistan. On returning, Sadiq reported to the Sheikh that Pakistan wanted to be an Islamic state. The Sheikh straightaway made up his mind and refused to accept any proposal which did not meet with his ethos of secularism. In 1932, Sheikh Abdullah along with Chaudhry Ghulam Abbas, had founded the All Jammu and Kashmir Muslim Conference, which was renamed the National Conference in 1939, in order to represent all the people of the state. The National Conference supported the accession of Kashmir to India. But in 1941, Ghulam Abbas broke away from the party and revived the old Muslim Conference, which supported the accession of Kashmir to Pakistan, and led the movement for Azad Kashmir.

That Sheikh Abdullah was confined to Kodaikanal in the south for twelve years is a story of misunderstanding. On 8 August 1953, Sheikh Abdullah was dismissed as the prime minister of Kashmir by the then Sadr-i-Riyasat (Constitutional Head of State) Dr Karan Singh, son of the erstwhile Maharaja Hari Singh, on the grounds that he had lost the support of the cabinet. He was not given a chance to prove his majority. Instead, he, along with Mirza Afzal Beg and twenty-two others, were accused of conspiracy against the state for allegedly espousing the cause of an independent Kashmir and were arrested soon after for anti-national activities. The 'Kashmir conspiracy case' was framed in 1958 and the trial began in 1959.

After two months' internment in Ooty, Sheikh Abdullah was taken to the Kohinoor bungalow, a few miles outside Kodaikanal, and remained under house arrest for more than a decade.

Even Sheikh Abdullah's personal friend, Jawaharlal Nehru, came to doubt him. The Sheikh's stand was that at the time of accession to India, Kashmir had given the centre only three subjects—defence, foreign affairs and communications—nothing more. All other subjects would be in the state's domain. Under the rules framed in 1947, in a federation like India the centre has sway over the subjects transferred by the states. It cannot unilaterally extend its authority to other subjects.

But in Kashmir, the central government wanted to usurp all the powers. This is what New Delhi has done and this has led to the Valley's alienation and hostility. Bodies like the Jan Sangh, the earlier incarnation of the Bharatiya Janata Party (BJP), and leaders like the late Shyama Prasad Mukerji, who died in a Jammu jail, used to insist that Kashmir must accede to India fully and become like any other state without any special status.

This, indeed, is the sad story of New Delhi's relations

with Sheikh Abdullah. When he opposed the centre's unilateral extension of authority over other subjects he was dismissed even though he had a majority of assembly members with him. According to Abdullah, his dismissal and arrest were ordered by the central government, headed by Jawaharlal Nehru. Some say his arrest was ordered by Nehru himself, others that he came to know of it only after the event.

On 8 April 1964, the state government dropped all charges in this infamous 'Kashmir conspiracy case'. Sheikh Abdullah was released and returned to Srinagar to an unprecedented welcome by the people of the Valley.

After his release he was reconciled with Nehru. Nehru requested Sheikh Abdullah to act as a bridge between India and Pakistan and make President Ayub Khan agree to come to New Delhi for talks for a final solution of the Kashmir problem. President Ayub also sent telegrams to Nehru and Sheikh Abdullah with the message that as Pakistan too was a party to the Kashmir dispute any resolution of the conflict without its participation would not be acceptable to Pakistan. This paved the way for Sheikh Abdullah's visit to Pakistan to help broker a solution to the Kashmir problem.

After the war with Pakistan in 1971, and the creation of Bangladesh, Sheikh Abdullah realized that for the survival of this region there was an urgent need to stop confrontational politics and resolve issues by a process of reconciliation and dialogue. When Nehru's daughter,

Indira Gandhi, came to power, the Sheikh started talks with her for normalizing the situation in the region, and came to an accord called the 1974 Indira–Sheikh accord, by giving up Kashmir's demand for a plebiscite (people's vote) in lieu of the people being given the right to self-rule by a democratically elected government rather than the puppet government which till then had ruled the state. Critics of Sheikh Abdullah hold the view that he gave up the cherished goal of a plebiscite for gaining the chief minister's chair. The National Conference won an overwhelming majority in the subsequent elections and re-elected Sheikh Abdullah as the chief minister in 1975. He remained as chief minister till his death in 1982.

Some laws which the Sheikh did not like were dropped. Many stayed because the Sheikh did not find them restricting the state's authority.

For example, the Sheikh found the extension of the Supreme Court's authority to be beneficial. He gladly supported it. But India's relentless bureaucratic efforts have since made several encroachments in the name of balanced rules and regulations. The fact is that New Delhi unilaterally extended several Indian laws without the state assembly's support.

The adverse fallout has been the alienation of Kashmiris. They feel cheated and have in growing numbers questioned even their state's fundamental accession to India. So we are back to the Partition formula even after some seventy years of independence.

10

Jayaprakash Narayan

Jayaprakash Narayan wasn't built to be a hero: slight of frame, racked by illness, battle-worn. Yet he was a tall man. He proved to be the outstanding hero who won us the second freedom in 1977, thirty years after the first one. Like Mahatma Gandhi, he tried to make us rise above our petty selves and acquire values while fighting for the protection of ideals. We did not measure up to his standard nor that of Gandhi. Our weaknesses have pulled us down. The fault is ours, not that of Mahatma Gandhi or JP.

Successive governments after Independence have done little to make political freedom meaningful, economically or socially. The white sahib has left and the brown sahib has sat in the chair. There is no change in the style or the content of governance. People find the authorities as oppressive as before and political leaders weak in performance.

Prime Minister Indira Gandhi mutilated the system even beyond recognition. For the first time she inducted an extra-constitutional authority to her government. This was her son, Sanjay Gandhi, who believed that India required autocracy, not democracy, for 'better and quicker' administration. One lakh people were detained without trial. High-handed and arbitrary actions were carried out with impunity. With the press gagged and an obedient bureaucracy, Sanjay Gandhi played havoc with the country.

Roughly two years before the Emergency, JP rang me up to invite me to inaugurate a students' meeting at Patna. I was then editor of the Delhi edition of *The Statesman*. I could never imagine that the meeting was a precursor of some type of revolution. A spark he kindled at that meeting would one day turn into a conflagration to consume the Indira Gandhi government which, in any case, had become too inept and too authoritarian.

JP called upon the youth to fight against undemocratic methods. He wanted them to be in the forefront to agitate for removal of ills that parties had injected into the country's body politic. Morality was the point he underlined. He was in favour of a partyless government, all political parties giving their shoulder to the task of building the country.

The meeting was a success in the sense that JP went from Bihar to Gujarat where the students' stir (Navnirman Andolan) forced the state government to quit. It was another matter that students like Lalu Yadav, who was in the chair at the meeting, derailed the movement when the Janata government assumed the reins of the government to rule single-handedly. The only morality they knew was how to capture power and to sustain it by hook or by crook. This was an antithesis of what JP stood for.

JP's movement was for cleansing. Was it possible to retrieve the nation which showed the best of its qualities of sacrifice and dedication during the struggle for Independence? Could he put it back on the road to idealism and values? Although the target was Mrs Gandhi's autocratic and corrupt rule, JP raised the larger question of propriety and morality in public life. Ultimately, the movement developed into the people's wrath against the mode of governance.

Strangely, the elite, including the intelligentsia, remained distant. Cocooned in its own way of comfortable living, it did not participate in what looked risky. No doubt it was disturbed over the concentration of power in the hands of Mrs Gandhi, Sanjay Gandhi and a few others. Even an ordinary policeman was seen to be a law unto himself. But the response of the elite was confined to drawing room tittle-tattle.

Most just caved in to the Emergency. In L.K. Advani's

words even the press which was asked to bend began to crawl. Never did even Sanjay Gandhi imagine that it would be so easy. JP was disappointed in his own way. He did not expect that the Congress, a party of his once-comrade, Jawaharlal Nehru, would go to the extent of suspending fundamental rights guaranteed by the Constitution. And he definitely expected more resistance from the thinking class.

There is a wrong assumption in certain quarters that the JP movement provoked Indira Gandhi to impose the Emergency. It is incorrect to believe that the Emergency was imposed to suppress the movement. Both were independent developments. What was common between the two was their failure. Both exposed the deficiencies of the society and the governing class. Mrs Gandhi imposed the Emergency not because there was a rightist combination building up to dislodge her. There was not a shred of evidence to support the thesis. She imposed it because after winning at the polls on the 'Garibi hatao' slogan in 1972, she was finding it difficult to govern. She had failed to deliver. People felt cheated. They were restive. She believed that the Allahabad High Court judgement to unseat her would consolidate the unrest.

The JP movement was a failure because it evoked very little response when the time came. As Mrs Gandhi put it, not even a dog barked. People were not inspired with lofty ideals of liberty and fair play to rise against her dictatorial ways. They were simply scared. However, they defeated her when the occasion arose. That was their catharsis.

At least some of JP's thoughts could have been implemented by the Janata government. It was his creature. It had been formed under his guidance as a vehicle for the broad spectrum of the opposition to Indira Gandhi. When Indira revoked the Emergency and called for elections in 1977, confident that she would win, it was a gross miscalculation on her part. The Janata party was voted into power and became the first non-Congress party to form a government at the centre. The victory was JP's. He had swept the polls and put a rag-tag combination in power. The Janata party government could have repaired the damage the Emergency had caused to the system and the institutions. Crime had been politicized and politics criminalized. There was no awareness of what was right, nor a desire to act according to what was right. Both public servants and politicians had lost their sense of duty. JP had asked the police not to obey illegal orders. But they had become a willing tool of tyranny which lasted nearly twenty months.

The post-Emergency government did little to restore the health of democracy except to make the re-imposition of Emergency difficult. Institutions were not helped to get back their vigour. Electoral reforms were necessary. A committee was formed to make recommendations. It did prepare a report but the government was not earnest about implementing them.

It is a tragedy that public servants or politicians who misused their power during the Emergency were never punished for the excesses they committed. The guilty changed colours overnight and sought a godfather within the Janata party. When Mrs Gandhi returned to power in 1980, the few public servants who had done their job honestly without staining their record were punished. The most telling effect of the Emergency was the general feeling which came to prevail that there was no line dividing right from wrong, moral from immoral.

The Janata government should have taken steps to restore the people's confidence in the rule of law. But its leaders got caught in power politics and petty personal quarrels. They had hardly any time, much less inclination, to make changes in the system which was reeking with crime and corruption. JP had wanted them to break the cartels of tainted politicians. Most had become part of it.

He found himself helpless. When he returned from America after medical treatment, he specially flew through Delhi. By then, the Janata government was a few months old. From the plane he looked at the tarmac. The airport was deserted. Having chosen Morarji Desai as the prime minister, even though Jagjivan Ram had a majority of the Lok Sabha members behind him, he was looking for Morarji. No one was there, not even JP's own devoted followers. He did not expect such a cold reception. Still he enquired whether Morarjibhai, Chaudhary Charan

Singh or Babu Jagjivan Ram were present at the airport. The government was represented by the tourism and civil aviation minister, Purushottam Kaushik. JP was visibly disappointed as he described the scene to me subsequently. He felt as if he had outlived his usefulness for the Janata the moment he put it on the gaddi.

As the Janata government went on bungling and as their internal bickering went on hitting the headlines, JP tried to intervene. He wanted to get some of them to Patna where he was lying sick. When I met him during those days, he was despondent and forlorn. Would Mrs Gandhi come back? I asked him in desperation. He said he didn't know. But one thing which he made clear was that she would never dare to impose the Emergency again.

On my return to Delhi, I met the prime minister and conveyed to him that JP felt neglected. Morarji lost his temper and snapped: 'Did he expect me to go to meet him? You know I never went to meet Gandhi. He is not taller than Gandhi.'

JP's real disappointment was not Morarji Desai whom he and Acharya Kripalani made the prime minister but the Sangh Parivar. He had permitted its members to join the movement on the promise that they would sever their links with the Rashtriya Swayamsevak Sangh (RSS), which he suspected was involved in the assassination of Mahatma Gandhi. Nathuram Godse, the killer, was an RSS member. Whenever JP would insist that the Jan Sangh members in the Janata party must officially disassociate themselves from the RSS, he was told that they were in the process of doing so. He felt cheated. He made no secret of the fact that they had gone back on their word. This was true. They had no intention of severing any connections with the RSS. Even after joining the Janata party, they stayed in touch with the RSS. They worked as a group although they were in different ministries. They did not want to renege on their promise in the lifetime of JP who they knew was very sick. Once he died, they appeared in their true colours.

When the Janata party came to consolidate its ranks, the Jan Sangh refused to cut off its ties with the RSS. The Janata's difference with the RSS was ideological. It saw the RSS as wanting to replace a pluralistic India with a Hindu Rashtriya. The Janata belatedly realized how the Jan Sangh members had used their two years' time in the government to penetrate not only the administrative machinery but the media, official and private.

It was obvious that the Jan Sangh members only wanted credibility which they did not have before the secular Janata party accommodated them under its umbrella. Once they got it, they formed a new party, the Bharatiya Janata Party, which played the Hindu card with a vengeance. JP realized that he had gone wrong in having taken them at their face value. But by then, he was dying. He had diabetes and a weak heart and had been on dialysis for kidney failure for some years.

Today when the Hindutva forces are gaining ground, it is a relief to see that Bihar, JP's state, is substantially free from it. But one of his staunch followers, Nitish Kumar, is now an ardent supporter of the BJP. George Fernandes, once JP's trusted hand, was the standard bearer of the BJP-led National Democratic Alliance (NDA) before he was struck down by illness.

We, human rights activists and civil liberty workers, cannot run away from blame. We have failed to stall the advance of saffronization. Even the areas where we have worked for years are not free from communalism. In Rajasthan where human rights activists have successfully won the right to information, the BJP has captured two-thirds of the state assembly seats. The places where we claim to have deepened our influence at the grassroots went totally to the BJP.

The point which we must consider is where we have gone wrong. Why is the saffronization reaching places where we are in touch with people all the time? Are we short in our commitment? In fact, the larger question which all human rights activists and civil liberty workers must face is why communalism is raising its ugly head when we have ostensibly gained some strength.

The obvious inference is that it is Mahatma Gandhi's sacrifice which saved us for more than four decades. The Sangh Parivar could not cross even the double digit figure in the Lok Sabha. Is it because of the contamination of the educated middle class? Is it the defeat of secular ideology at the hands of communal entities?

Whatever the reason, we cannot minimize our failure. We must analyse why we have not been able to convince the people among whom we have worked that parochialism and sectarianism come in the way of their own welfare and that of the country's development. I hope that our own ranks of human rights activism are free from the taint of communalism and casteism.

While taking stock of our work and approach, we should ask ourselves: is it sufficient to confine ourselves to the fieldwork? Why have we been shunning elections? Is it because of fear of losing? Is it enough that, at time of polling, we have taken interest in elections and voted for non-BJP forces because they, we believe, are a lesser evil?

Let us admit that there is no running away from the polls in a democratic set-up. If we want a peaceful transition in the country, we, the activists and civil rights workers, have to get into Parliament and state assemblies. We cannot sit back and see the misuse of power by those who have no faith in the ideals we pursue or the changes we want to bring about.

I concede that it will take us long to win a majority but even then the presence of some of us in Parliament and the state assemblies will make the difference. At present we run after MPs and MLAs to ensure that our voice is heard at the places where the decisions are taken. While in the

Rajya Sabha, I recall that the briefing by Aruna Roy from Rajasthan helped me in the parliamentary committee on home affairs to have amendments made in the legislation on the Right to Information.

Although JP favoured a partyless government, he conceded that there had to be a government which would need to be captured through elections. He proved it after the Emergency by sweeping the polls. Mahatma Gandhi used the Congress party as his instrument for the struggle to oust the British. We should have some platform, some forum, which people come to identify with clean and credible alternatives. It will be tough going but we should be prepared for failures in the beginning. In the process we may initiate some thinking among the Naxalites and other similar groups that power will not come through the mouth of cannons but through the elected bodies which wield power.

Many may find such efforts confusing and feel that elections may divert our attention from the real problem. There is no more pressing problem than making people free from poverty. The state power is necessary for any meaningful efforts to do so. If the nation is to preserve the fundamental values of a democratic society, there is no option. The JP movement ultimately had to capture power.

But, how do we ensure that the people sent to Parliament and the state assemblies do not behave the way in which the Janata party did? There will have to be two wings—one consisting of those who are engaged in the legislative business and the other of those who do constructive work. Both should be answerable to a central body. Mahatma Gandhi pursued the same line when leading the struggle for Independence.

While shuttling between Patna and Mumbai for medical treatment, JP realized the necessity of reconstructing something different. He did not have many days to go. He was confined to Patna. It was only his indomitable spirit that had kept him alive, not only physically but also mentally.

He telephoned me one day in 1979. I was then working at the *Indian Express*. He sounded as healthy as I had found him when he rang me up to inaugurate the students' meeting at Patna. He asked me to meet him. He said he would invite some more people, specially economists, to think afresh. Ideologies, he said, had failed to find an answer to the country's problems. Something new had to be done and soon. He admitted that neither socialism, nor any other 'ism' would bring the desired result. There should be a new economic policy to give priority to the basic problems of people.

JP wanted real social and economic progress to usher in and believed that it would not happen until the opportunity was given to an ordinary man and woman to develop. The touchstone was how far any political or social theory made the individual rise above his petty self and think in terms of the good of all.

Strange, Jawaharlal Nehru made the same point in a lecture on 'India's Today and Tomorrow'. He said: 'We talk of the welfare state and of democracy. They are good concepts but they hardly convey a clear and unambiguous meaning. Democracy and socialism are means to an end, not the end by themselves. We talk of the good of society. Is this something apart from and transcending the good of the individuals composing it? If the individual is ignored and sacrificed for what is considered the good of society, is that the right objective to have?'

JP admitted that Marxism had thrown considerable light on the economic process but was in many ways out of date. His purpose of inviting me and some others was to do our own thinking. JP was essentially trying to find a path which was suited to India's genius. I could not respond to his call quickly enough. When I reached Patna, it was too late. He had passed away by then.

11

B.P. Koirala

My interest in Nepal began from the day B.P. Koirala, founder of the Nepali Congress, called me from the All India Medical Sciences Institute (AIIMS), where he had been lying ill for several weeks. Koirala had served as the prime minister of Nepal for eighteen months before he was diagnosed with cancer and was obliged to seek treatment first in New Delhi and later in the US.

It was in the late 1960s that Koirala sent me a message from AIIMS, explaining he was awaiting treatment but would be happy to see me at my convenience. At the time I was heading the UNI news agency and my column was appearing in the *Kathmandu Post* and other Nepalese newspapers.

My support for a liberal and sovereign Nepal appealed to him and he wanted to personally thank me. It was around noon that I made the trip to his hospital bed where he was lying alone in the room. Indian doctors were treating him but it was an open secret that the US was interested in his welfare and an American embassy doctor had visited him two or three times to find out more about his condition and the treatment he was undergoing. Some years later, the US State Department arranged for him to travel to Boston for further medical checks and continued treatment at the hands of their own specialists.

The significance of the US interest in Koirala underlined their belief in the importance of Nepal as a listening post for South Asia, China and other surrounding areas. To this end they installed a powerful radio transmitter in the region, ostensibly to broadcast Voice of America bulletins, but also to record anything of significance. Among those who were alarmed by this style of electronic surveillance was Congress president K. Kamaraj who lodged a formal protest at this intrusion. The Americans declined to comment and this remains their position till today. Their listening devices remain intact.

The US influence in Nepal did not come up in my discussions that afternoon with Koirala. What we talked about was how the future of Nepal should be defined in liberal, democratic terms. Then and later Nepal's political inspiration came from India's Constitution and the early years of our freedom struggle. Both Koirala and his family were loyal supporters of Mahatma Gandhi. He himself was a graduate of two Indian universities and spent many years of exile in Benares. He too supported peaceful non-violent protests and just like Indian Congress party leaders, he too was imprisoned by the British colonial authorities who accused him of having contacts with terrorists.

Back in Nepal he was far more popular than all other leaders put together. A handsome man, simple in the way he dressed, he appealed to the ordinary Nepali because of his selflessness and his relentless fight against the hereditary Ranas who had been de facto rulers of their country for more than a hundred years. By helping to overthrow the last Rana, Koirala paved the way for the return of the popular monarch in the shape of King Tribhuvan Bir Bikram Shah. But Nepal could not have two parallel centres of power and Koirala only lasted for eighteen months before he was forced into exile across the border in India.

In my conversation with Koirala, we did touch upon his experiences with the colonial authorities, the monarch and his kinship with India. It soon became obvious that a huge reservoir of goodwill for India existed with Koirala and his Nepalese Congress Party colleagues. They were all Hindus who drew their inspiration from India.

Now that China is trying to befriend Nepal, it is easy to forget the easy-going relationship that used to exist in the past between New Delhi and Kathmandu. Some of that still survives, but with the Chinese Yuan flowing so fast and free, Nepalese leaders can as easily go for treatment to Beijing as they can to New Delhi. Of course, the one advantage we have is the soft border, something the Chinese cannot match, that allows Nepalese and Indian citizens to freely travel between the two countries.

Surprisingly, Koirala was not bitter against the king whom he referred to as the 'Maharaj'. In fact, he wanted him to have a place in the country's polity although his own personal preference was for popular democratic rule.

At one time Nepal wanted to be part of India when King Tribhuvan had also taken shelter in India as the popular mood at the time in Nepal was for a constitutional monarchy. The king's offer to merge with India reflected the popular mood, but it was rejected by Prime Minister Jawaharlal Nehru who was acutely aware of the need for a buffer state between India and China. I was surprised when I came to know of this. I checked the story with Koirala, who said that Nehru was clear in his mind that Nepal should stay as a sovereign state, democratic, with a freely elected Parliament. Nehru did however, emphasize that the two countries should have soft borders and plans for a close military and economic relationship.

Subsequently, when I visited Nepal, I found people voicing various grievances that had taken the shape of an anti-India feeling. I would apportion blame for this to Delhi's foreign affairs ministry. Its envoy in Kathmandu, operating from a massive embassy, behaved in an imperialistic way, just like the British viceroys who ruled India for 150 years. In much the same way, New Delhi expected Kathmandu to seek guidance from our ministry of foreign affairs, dabbling in Nepal's internal politics.

This attitude boomeranged and took an ugly shape when the monarchy was overthrown and the king became only a figurehead. India's bid to maintain indirect rule was so much resented that Nepal came to tilt towards Maoist China. Nehru's assurance that 'We have taken particular care not to interfere' took a contrary shape. Since then, despite the cultural and religious ties with India, Nepal has gone out of its way to cultivate Pakistan.

The 1953 bilateral treaty which New Delhi had signed with Kathmandu was loaded in favour of India and defined security relations as if Nepal was India's vassal. Although both countries want to get away from the legacy of the past, the 1953 treaty still hangs like an albatross round our necks. India's short-sighted policies have alienated Nepal to such an extent that it has begun a relationship of proximity with China. This may not work in the long run because Nepal's religion and heritage are so intertwined with India that Kathmandu psychologically and emotionally depends on the people in India, particularly UP and Bihar.

Prime Minister Narendra Modi visited Nepal in 2014 to repair the relationship. But Kathmandu continues to play the China card to get money from both New Delhi and Beijing. The situation does not look like changing. Until there is an alteration, both India and Nepal will continue to be distant neighbours.

12

J.R.D. Tata

Jehangir Ratanji Dadabhoy Tata, better known as JRD, put the Tatas on the world map. JRD was persuasive, conciliatory and reticent. In contrast, his successor Ratan Tata, doesn't believe so much in methods as in results. Although not in politics, he tries to influence those who are at the helm of important parties. To my mind, he is not a patch on JRD.

When it comes to the media, the approach of JRD was markedly different. I was resident editor of *The Statesman* in Delhi when JRD, at the instance of Jawaharlal Nehru, constituted a consortium of businessmen to buy the newspaper from a British company. I found JRD always diffident about his association with the paper. He told me many a time that he had more troubles with *The Statesman* than in his other businesses put together though he had only eight per cent of shares in the paper.

For a certain generation of Indians JRD's name will forever be synonymous with Air India, India's international carrier, symbolized by the welcoming Maharaja whose tilted head and turban was associated with the welcoming generosity of India's royal families. British Airways (earlier BOAC and before that, Imperial Airways) had a Speedbird logo first used in 1932. Australia's Qantas uses a kangaroo, so Air India's welcoming Maharaja was something different and unique among the world's national airlines.

JRD's friends and critics alike say he was almost obsessed with the airline, spending huge amounts of time on its aircraft as they travelled to different destinations. He took a personal interest in the internal décor, the types of uniforms worn by the pilots, even the saris issued to the air hostesses. If the crockery and cutlery used on the aircraft were not his liking, JRD had them sent back without any compunction.

Although the Maharaja mascot had to be approved by JRD, it was actually the creation of Air India's first commercial director, Bobby Kooka. A leading member of Bombay's Parsi community, like JRD, Kooka was quoted as saying about the Maharaja, 'We call him a Maharaja for want of a better description. But his blood isn't blue. He may look like royalty, but he isn't royal.'

Despite his wealth, JRD was both simple and frugal in his day to day habits. Visitors invited to his Bombay home always commented on his modest clothes and eating habits, typical of the world's extremely wealthy. He had plenty of money but didn't see the need to brag about it.

Apart from Air India and his many and varied industrial investments which made him one of the world's richest men, JRD was also the owner of Bombay's legendary Taj Mahal hotel. This, too, was associated with a gracious and lavish style of living that visitors often commented upon. Its large rooms and washrooms, long corridors that seemed to go on for miles and wonderful and varied cuisine all seemed to belong to a bygone age. Yet it lacked that final magic touch that Air India seemed to have in bucketloads. JRD was once asked why he didn't spend as much time on the Taj as he did with Air India, and he replied he would not know where to begin.

A nephew of JRD and his chosen successor, Ratan Tata filed a petition before the Supreme Court to protect the privacy of his company and family, one of his few good endeavours. JRD would have supported the cause because he, too, was a very private person. However, I have not liked Ratan Tata's association with the PR firm headed by Niira Radia. He has for the first time pushed the Tatas into the realm of lobbies, pressures and contacts. JRD would not have sanctioned such a thing.

Whatever his compulsions, Ratan Tata has done one good thing. I am referring to his disclosure about the connection of the media with the corporate world. One of his affidavits contended that the *Outlook* magazine is the property of a real estate owner. Ratan Tata has also given the details of money invested by some others in the corporate sector in leading TV channels. An inquiry has to be made into these allegations because the freedom of expression is involved. Even a probe by the Press Council of India will be inadequate. The media has to be above suspicion. There are so many channels, running with dubious funds, that the council should be allowed to find out who finances who and how.

The question of individuals' privacy which Ratan Tata had raised concerns us all. Increasingly, the government is curbing the freedom of people in the name of danger from terrorism and such other militant avenues. But the government agencies have spread themselves so much all over that they are now even peeping through keyholes to know what is happening inside the boardrooms. That the Supreme Court is seized of the matter sustains hope that it would draw the Laxman rekha, which the government agencies on the one hand, and people on the other, should respect.

Tapping phones is a legal invasion by the government on private persons. I consider it immoral and against the spirit of the Constitution. But then the government has got the authority under the law. The problem with the government agencies is that they find it difficult to let go of the authoritarianism which they enjoyed during the Emergency. They do not seem to realize that the privacy of individuals is sacrosanct in a democratic society.

Ratan Tata's complaint that an inquiry should be made into the alleged disclosure of the Radia tapes by the Central Bureau of Investigation (CBI) carries weight. It is not a secret that the agency is a department of the government of India. Therefore, everything it does, however laudable, is at the end of a telephone call by a top official or a minister. The BJP used the CBI as much as the ruling Congress was doing. Therefore, Ratan Tata is quite right to demand an independent agency to look into the violation of an individual's privacy.

This may well be a good opportunity for the government to make the CBI an autonomous organization like the Central Election Commission (CEC), which is answerable only to Parliament. This matter came before the Parliamentary Standing Committee some six years ago when I was its member. But the ruling BJP had opposed it then. The Congress, too, did not favour the proposal to make the CBI independent. Governments of all hues want the agencies to be pliable for other purposes.

13

Khushwant Singh

I called him Professor Sahib. He had taught me company law in my final year at Law College in Lahore where I was studying for an LL.B degree. He was a bar-at-law from London and was a popular lecturer because he never stopped any student from leaving the classroom whenever he or she wanted.

After Partition I lost contact with him till we met at a voice test for an All India Radio post. I had come to give the test. Khushwant was a senior journalist at AIR, and was conducting the test. He rejected me because I could not pronounce some words properly in English. During his stint at Akashvani, our relationship changed from that of teacher and student, to one of friends. The age difference between us was only a few years. However, by then he had become a celebrated author and had written a two-volume book on Sikh history for the United Nations Educational, Scientific and Cultural Organization (UNESCO).

Although he wrote strongly against Jarnail Singh Bhindranwale during the militancy in Punjab in the late 1960s and the early 1970s, he returned the Padma Bhushan award after Operation Bluestar, when Indira Gandhi had ordered the army to storm the Golden Temple in Amritsar. He was against all that Bhindranwale stood for but he could not condone the attack on the Darbar Sahib, the Sikh community's Vatican. No doubt, he was secular and vehemently opposed all those who preached parochialism. Yet he did not want the entire community to be targeted for the sins of a few extremists.

He used to write a weekly column, 'With Malice Towards One and All' and minced no words to assail the militants in Punjab. Still, during the anti-Sikh riots in 1984, he had to seek shelter in the Swiss embassy in the Diplomatic Enclave in Delhi to escape the wrath of the Hindu extremists who were killing the Sikhs with the connivance of the police.

There were times when he allowed personal loyalty to outweigh the wrongs of a situation. He supported Indira Gandhi during the Emergency, more so Sanjay Gandhi, an extra-constitutional authority. His proximity to them was on account of Sanjay's wife, Maneka, a distant relation. Khushwant Singh was dubbed 'Khushamat Singh', because he echoed Indira Gandhi's thoughts. This was not due to a sharing of ideology, but to the blind support he extended to Sanjay.

Khushwant Singh never forgot a friend. After my stint in jail during the Emergency, I met him at Mumbai. He had heard that the *Indian Express*, where I was working, might sack me because of my anti-Sanjay views. He voluntarily offered me a column in the *Illustrated Weekly* of which he was the editor. He told me that the remuneration for the column would be enough to cover my expenses if and when I lost my job. That eventuality did not arise because the owner of the *Indian Express*, Ram Nath Goenka, then stood by me like a rock.

Yet Goenka, too, faltered when the return of Indira Gandhi looked certain. He took me along to meet Khushwant Singh. I did not know that Goenka had offered him the chief editorship of the *Express*. Khushwant, already feeling unhappy in the *Times of India* group, took no time to say 'yes'. I, who was the go-between, was to intimate Khushwant Singh about the date when he would take over the paper.

Before he could join, I got a scoop that the Emergency would be lifted and new elections held. Goenka used to see the front page at midnight before going to sleep. He read the story and rang me up to ask me not to contact Khushwant Singh. Soon after, Khushwant called me to ask when he was expected to join the *Express*. I told him that Goenka had changed his mind. Khushwant Singh rightly felt betrayed.

What was most endearing about Khushwant Singh was that he had an open house. All of us, no matter how high or low our status, Hindus and people of different faiths, men and women, would congregate at his place in Sujan Singh Park in south Delhi in the evening and enjoy his conversation and hospitality. He was, however, strict about timings. Everybody had to clear out by 8 p.m. since he went to bed early, woke up at four in the morning, made tea for himself and sat at his desk to write. That was the time when he did most of his writing.

He has authored numerous books, including some novels, and most of them have been translated in other languages. His very name sold because he had an inimitable style which people liked. He would talk about the most intricate problem in an easy understandable way, which an ordinary person understood.

In February 2014, we, his friends and admirers, gathered together to make a documentary on him to celebrate his hundredth birthday which would be in August that year. He was then ninety-nine. Little did we know that he would pass away barely two months later, on 20 March, just a few months short of his centenary. When I went to his house after his demise and touched his feet, I was forlorn. I still feel his absence. There are not many who can withstand the constant criticism for standing up for pluralism. A small statue of Lord Buddha in the shelf behind his chair probably told it all. Did he believe in spiritualism or Sufism, or both? He told me many a time that he was an agnostic. Yet God created him in his own image. Khushwant Singh will always be remembered for his writing, his scholarship, his great generosity of spirit, and the democratic, secular principles he held on to till the end.

14

Meena Kumari and Noor Jehan

Meena Kumari was at the height of her success as an actress when Lal Bahadur Shastri, then home minister, was invited to the shooting of *Pakeezah*, in which she was the heroine. She played the lead role of a golden-hearted nautch girl from Lucknow. Raaj Kumar, Ashok Kumar and Nadira were also in the film. The pressure to attend came from the Maharashtra chief minister and it was so strong that Shastri could not say no.

The function was held in a film studio at Bombay where *Pakeezah* was being shot, and was attended by leading personalities from the cinema world. Many top actors were present. Meena Kumari garlanded Shastri. Amidst loud applause, Shastri asked me in his soft voice who the lady was. Meena Kumari, I said in amazement. Shastri expressed his ignorance. Yet never did I expect him to admit this in public.

But, all credit to Shastri's innocence and honesty. He began his speech with the remark: 'Meena Kumariji, mujhe maaf karna, maine aapka naam pahle dafa suna hai' (Meena Kumariji, please forgive me, I have heard your name for the first time). The legendary beauty of Hindi cinema, the darling of millions across the nation, was a figure of embarrassment and sat impassively in the front row.

Shastri was given a tour of the film studio. For him, it was like going through a routine exercise. Shastri's speech made no comment about the sets or the film itself. The reality is that *Pakeezah* turned out to be a big commercial success and went on to become a cult classic. Meena Kumari's reputation climbed to greater heights.

Despite all the adulation from her fans, Meena Kumari, born Mahjabeen Bano, always felt insecure at the top. People distanced themselves from her out of awe. She was the third wife of the film director, Kamal Amrohi, known for his perfectionism and exacting standards. Kamal Amrohi's first wife, Bilkis Bano, was said to be a maid of Nargis' mother, Jaddan Bai. His second wife was Mehmoodie. Meena Kumari met him on the sets of *Tamasha*, in 1951, when they were introduced by Ashok Kumar. Amrohi offered her a role in his upcoming film, *Anarkali*. Soon after signing the contract, Meena Kumari met with a serious car accident and spent four months in hospital. It was in hospital that her love affair with Amrohi blossomed. They continued to meet after she was discharged from hospital, and on 14 February 1952, they secretly got married in a simple nikah ceremony in the presence of a qazi and Meena Kumari's younger sister, Mahliqa. She was only eighteen, and Kamal Amrohi was thirty-four, an already married man with three children from his previous wife.

The marriage was not a happy one. Amrohi was abusive and controlling, and exploited Meena Kumari for his films. Meena Kumari sought refuge in other men and developed infatuations for one person after another. Dharmendra was the one with whom she fell head over heels in love. On the other hand, Dharmendra was casual, definitely not emotionally involved. She took to drink to forget him and moved from one peg of whisky to one bottle.

As Meena Kumari sank deeper into alcoholism, she was unable to come to the sets, and Amrohi had to suspend the shooting of *Pakeezah*. By the time he resumed shooting, Meena Kumari had put on weight and her face was no longer the beautiful chiselled countenance that had captured the imagination of hundreds of movie-goers. As she was his wife plus a leading star, Amrohi had no option but to continue using her in the film. But he laid down certain humiliating conditions to which Meena Kumari had to agree. They were as follows:

1. You will return home by 6.30 every evening.
2. You will allow no one in the make-up room except your make-up man.
3. You will sit in your own car which will take you to work and bring you back.

Meena Kumari agreed on paper to all the terms but kept on breaking them. She was watched over and followed by Kamal Amrohi's men. He had issued strict instructions to keep an eye on her and had deployed his assistant, Baqar Ali, to prevent any other man from meeting Meena Kumari on the sets.

It is said by her supporters that Meena Kumari felt oppressed at the feudal and high-handed behaviour that Kamal Amrohi brought to their relationship. It was a complex relationship, not least because Kamal Amrohi's lavish productions, *Daera* and *Pakeezah*, and his Kamalistan studios, were mostly financed by Meena Kumari's earnings.

From its mahurat on 18 January 1958, to its release on 4 February 1972, *Pakeezah* took fourteen years to reach the silver screen. Meena Kumari attended the last premiere of her life along with Kamal Amrohi. Already battling cirrhosis of the liver, she was ill throughout the filming and died only a few weeks after it was released.

Meena Kumari could not jettison her love for Dharmendra. When she died there was a photo of

Dharmendra on the opposite wall. It is said that Amrohi's own brother, a wealthy businessman, got her killed because of the shame she had brought to the family. This consideration may have made him have her killed, despite her standing as an actress. To this day whenever I go to Bombay I recall how a great actress died in a state of misery that she brought upon herself.

○

Just as Meena Kumari was an icon of Bollywood in India, so was Noor Jehan the darling of the masses in Pakistan. I have Prime Minister Zulfikar Ali Bhutto's staff to thank for getting the opportunity to meet her. I was in Lahore and on my way to Islamabad to interview Bhutto and, as his guest, the local information department was on its toes to please me. They asked me if there was anything in particular that I wanted.

It so happened that I had studied at Lahore, first at Forman Christian College for my graduation and then at Law College for the LL.B degree. Even otherwise, I was a frequent visitor to Lahore. Sialkot city was my home town and Lahore was the place where I did my studies after matriculation. The local information staff asked if I would like to revisit my old haunts in the city, but I replied in the negative.

What I did have an appetite for was the opportunity to meet singer and actress Noor Jehan. My hosts were surprised. They made telephone calls to locate her and finally found her at a film studio in Model Town in Lahore.

She was recording a song when we reached the place. After she had finished they ushered me into a room where two ladies were sitting. Both were generously proportioned, nothing like my childhood recall of the slim and glamorous star from yesteryears. My memory of Noor Jehan was from the days when she was Baby Noor Jehan. Her voice, which even Lata Mangeshkar envied, had captured the heart of the entire subcontinent.

Which of the two was Noor Jehan? The two ladies looked alike, and I could not identify which of them was the one I was looking for. My guide nudged me and pointed to the woman on the right. I greeted her with a salaam as she offered me a seat next to her.

It took some time to recognize the plump-faced woman as Noor Jehan. Because of her status as a star and an icon, I felt a bit shy to initiate the conversation. My first somewhat predictable question was to ask how many songs she had recorded. Her instant reply swept me off my feet. She said: 'Na he gaano ka shamaar hai aur na hi gunaho ka' (Neither can I remember the number of records nor count the number of sins I have committed). The first one you would forgive and the second was up to Allah, she added. No, she was not trying to be modest. She really felt insecure whenever one of her records was released. Every time she recorded a song she felt as if she was appearing in an exam where she might fail.

I wanted her to sing *Heer*, the Punjabi's obsession. She was not in the mood. She asked me when I was visiting my home town. I told her the next day. For my sake, she then arranged the screening of a film show where she had sung *Heer*. The cinema hall was situated on the road to Sialkot. This was where we stopped roughly before noon. It was blazing hot outside but the cinema was properly air conditioned. Apart from my security escort, I was the only viewer in the entire hall. This was her special gift for me and I have never forgotten the gesture.

15

Faiz Ahmad Faiz

We were a team of visiting Indian journalists having breakfast in a restaurant near the Kremlin in Moscow, when a middle-aged person of medium height entered the dining room. It was only Inder Malhotra who recognized him, then got up from his seat to say: 'Gentlemen, let us honour the greatest living poet in the subcontinent.'

This was the first time I saw Faiz Ahmad Faiz. I was a passionate follower of Urdu poetry, had read him a lot and admired his commitment to the cause of the downtrodden. To this day it is his poetry that still inspires. UNESCO is one of the many international institutions that honoured him by bringing out his poems.

One sample reads:

Only a few days, dear one, a few days more
Under oppression's shadows condemned to breathe,
Still for a time we must bear them, and tears, and
    endure
What our forefathers, not our own faults, bequeath
Fettered limbs, each impulse held on a chain,
Minds in bondage, our words all watched and set
    down.
Courage still nerves us, or how should we still exist,
Now with existence only a beggar's gown,
Tattered, and patched every hour with new rags of
    pain?
Yes, but to tyranny not many hours are left now;
Patience a little, few hours of lamenting remain.
In this parched air of an age that desert sands choke
We must stay now—not forever and ever stay!
Under this load beyond words of a foreign yoke
We must submit for a while—not forever submit!
Dust of affliction that clings to your beauty today,
Crosses unnumbered that mar our few mornings of
    youth,
Torment of silver nights, a pain with no cure,
Heartache unanswered, the body's long cry of despair—
Only a few days, dear one, a few days more.

UNESCO has rendered a great service by translating Faiz
into English. This enables those who do not know Urdu to
appreciate the value of his work. Woefully, the translation
does not do justice to his great poetry. Understandably,

the flavour of language cannot be fully captured. But what the translation misses is the height Faiz attains with his thoughts and the pathos of the common man he brings out. His poetry urges you to revolt against the system and appeals to you to oust it lock, stock and barrel.

Subsequently, I heard him reciting his poems at the annual mushaira, or gathering of poets, hosted by Delhi Cloth Mills. However, his vocal rendering was prosaic and did not match the heights of his written poetry.

Some of his devoted followers agreed there was a seeming contradiction between the dizzying heights he attained as a poet of international stature and his earlier years of service with the British Indian army during World War II. He served in the army until 1947 when he resigned to become editor of the English language *Civil and Military Gazette* newspaper, later renamed as the *Pakistan Times*. It was during the war years that he met and married his English wife, Alys, who subsequently became a Pakistani national. The couple had two daughters, Saleema and Moneeza.

When I came to know him personally through my friends and fellow lovers of Urdu, Sheila and Hali, I asked him who best had rendered his poems in music. Faiz took no time in saying: 'Nur Naria', a famous Pakistani singer of that time.

I thought he would mention Iqbal Bano, another famous singer of the subcontinent who had brought so much emotion to the singing of his poems. But Faiz had a different yardstick. Nur Naria was the one he preferred over all others.

We must have met each other about thirty times when we greeted each other and I would listen to him rendering his 'kalaam'. When we had longer discussions we talked about the tragedy of Partition, India and Pakistan and the glory of the Urdu language. Then we discovered we had something else in common, since we both came from Sialkot, also the birthplace of another Urdu icon in the shape of Allama Iqbal.

The secession of East Pakistan in 1971 affected Faiz in many ways. One, he did not forgive India for having militarily assisted the rebellion. A man of the people, he reacted adversely to the revolt of people in East Pakistan. On the one hand he hailed their liberation movement, but on the other hand he did not want to support a movement that ended in the break up of Pakistan. It was clear that nationalism had the better of him. He not only regretted the liberation but denounced those who broke Pakistan.

Like so many other profound thinkers and poets from around the world, he thoroughly enjoyed his drink. Wherever he went, his hosts were told that 'a full bottle' of Scotch should be available for him. It was amazing that he would not falter in reciting, even after finishing the bottle. Black Dog was his favourite and his admirers who invited him to their homes knew that.

Some people, finicky about his pronunciation, would remark that he recited his Urdu poetry in a Punjabi accent. Once he got so exasperated by such remarks that he switched over to reciting his poetry in Punjabi. His critics had to plead with him to return to Urdu.

Leftist in ideology, Faiz, like other comrades, was frugal in personal habits and living. He did not ask anyone for a fee. His books did very well and earned him handsome royalties. Where he did demand payment was at the mushairas he was invited to attend across the subcontinent. He was always being invited to one place or another where his personal expenditure was very low but he would insist that his accompanying artistes and musicians be paid. I often dropped him back at his friend's house in New Delhi on these occasions. Whether in India or abroad, his friends were mostly non-Muslims.

Faiz did not believe in any religion. His humanity was his religion. But since he lived in Pakistan, he talked about Islam which he described as Lal Islam, or 'Red' Islam. His supporters deny he was a communist, but admit he was a camp follower of Pakistan's communist party,

His ideological convictions were respected by fellow leftist Zulfikar Ali Bhutto who was the foreign minister and later prime minister of Pakistan. When Faiz was sentenced to four years in prison for his alleged complicity in a failed coup, it was Bhutto who championed his cause by facilitating his appointment to the National Council of the Arts. When Bhutto himself was overthrown and later executed in 1979 by General Zia-ul-Haq, Faiz fled to exile in Beirut where he lived until 1982. He returned home to Lahore where he survived for another two years until his death in 1984, shortly after being nominated for the Nobel Prize for literature.

16

Atal Bihari Vajpayee

After Partition, travel restrictions were imposed between India and Pakistan, and most rail and road links were closed. This made it virtually impossible for families who had relatives on both sides of the border, to meet each other. It was a tragic aftermath of the bloodshed of 1947. Finally, in 1976, a train service, the Samjhauta Express, was started between the two countries to permit divided families to visit their relatives, and to foster commerce and tourism.

In 1999, a bus service was also started between Delhi and Lahore. Officially known as Sada-e-Sarhad, the Delhi–Lahore bus service was a key element in the efforts of the Indian and Pakistani governments to improve the frosty and tense relations after the 1998 Pokhran nuclear tests in India, and the immediate Pakistani response of the Chagai

Hills tests. In its inaugural run on 19 February 1999, the bus carried Prime Minister Atal Bihari Vajpayee, on his way to attend a summit in Lahore at the invitation of his Pakistani counterpart, Nawaz Sharif.

I was a member of the delegation accompanying Vajpayee, and was seated behind him in the bus. Just before we reached the Wagah border, fifteen kilometres from Amritsar, Vajpayee beckoned me to his side and showed me a telegram. It contained the message that some twenty-six Hindus had been killed by militants in Jammu and Kashmir. Vajpayee spoke in anguish and wondered whether there was any use in further talks. My argument was that the militants were desperate to stall the dialogue with Nawaz Sharif and that they committed murders to provoke the Hindus. He saw the point but was not sure how the Indian public would react to the visit despite the killings.

A worried Vajpayee entered Pakistan amid festivities on both sides of the border. Nawaz Sharif was waiting at Wagah to receive him. The welcome ceremony was short and simple. The three service chiefs of Pakistan were present but did not salute Vajpayee. He and Nawaz Sharif flew to Lahore in a helicopter while I and the rest of the delegation continued the journey in the same bus.

The journey reminded me of the days of Partition when I had walked from my home in Sialkot, to Lahore. Now I was in a vehicle covering the same road between

Amritsar and Lahore. But this time there were no dead bodies, burnt vehicles or scattered luggage. Men and women standing in fields or in front of their houses waved at us vigorously. We waved back. There was hardly any difference between this countryside and the one which we had left behind in India.

In Lahore we were put up in the five-star Pearl Continental hotel. After changing hurriedly we made our way to the governor's house where Vajpayee was staying, where we waited for him to join us before proceeding to the banquet at the Qila (Fort). It was a long wait of more than two hours and nobody told us the reason for the delay. Ultimately, Vajpayee, along with his secretary and others, emerged from the building. Only then did we come to know that the road to the Fort had been literally taken over by the radical Jamaat-e-Islami. Its members and supporters had turned back all vehicles and had even stoned some cars carrying diplomats.

As we travelled down the road, we could see piles of bricks stacked on both sides. Shabaz Sharif, chief minister of Pakistan's Punjab, told me that the Jamaat had promised to protest for only a few minutes as a symbolic exercise but they had played false. I imagined that an agreement was probably the only way out because the Jamaat had a strong presence in Lahore.

Vajpayee read out his banquet speech in English. It was deadly dull with no life. It was obvious that it had been pieced together by some bureaucrats. These were the same bureaucrats who had at one time decided that the leaders of different political parties would accompany Vajpayee to Lahore. When I came to know about it, I prevailed upon Vajpayee's principal secretary, Brajesh Mishra, that the prime minister would get a better reception if he were to be accompanied by eminent artists, writers and scientists so that Pakistan should get the message from this gesture that Vajpayee had the backing of the intelligentsia. So our delegation included some celebrities from Hindi cinema—Dev Anand, Javed Akhtar and Shatrughan Sinha—cricketer Kapil Dev and dancer and theatre artiste Mallika Sarabhai.

Sadly, Vajpayee's speech was as much a disaster as would have been the delegation of politicians. Even if there was a message, it was lost in the involved sentences and familiar clichés. The only relieving part was the elaborately decorated Fort, the shaded light silhouetting large trees and lush green lawns.

The following morning I met Vajpayee and told him that his speech at the civic reception later in the day should be in his own words drawn both from Urdu and Hindi. He agreed and his words went down so well that even today people recall that speech with nostalgia. He told the audience that Pakistan did not need anyone's recognition because it had its own entity and recognition. Earlier, he had written in the visitors' book at Minar-e-Pakistan, the place where the Lahore Resolution was passed, that the integrity and prosperity of India depended upon the integrity and prosperity of Pakistan.

Vajpayee's speech was received with such emotional goodwill that some Pakistanis told me afterwards, 'If your prime minister stood for election today over here, he would sweep the polls.'

At lunch, while the two prime ministers were busy talking, the Pakistan delegation was hosted by Sahabzada Yakub (Khan), once Pakistan's foreign minister. Both of us sat at the same table. The conversation turned out to be meaningful. He asked the person sitting next to me to which place he belonged. His reply was North-West Frontier Province. Sahabzada's next question was: How did he see Kashmir? A distant land which did not interest him in one way or the other, was the reply. A similar response came from two other persons sitting at the table. One of them was from Sind and the other from Baluchistan. Sahabzada turned towards me and said: 'This (Kashmir) is your problem (meaning, of the Punjabis on both sides), you should settle it. Why get others from both countries involved?'

The outcome of the summit was that Vajpayee and Nawaz Sharif signed the Lahore Declaration, which pledged both nations to the peaceful resolution of bilateral disputes, especially that of the Kashmir conflict and deployment of nuclear weapons, while fostering friendly commercial and cultural relations. A friend of mine, Mushahid Hussain, was Vajpayee's minister-in-waiting. He, a hardliner, was positive about the Declaration. He told me later that it was the best thing that could happen to the two countries. There was a road map for the settlement of Kashmir as well as a time frame. He did not give me any details of what had transpired between the two prime ministers during the discussions that led up to the Declaration.

Little did I know at that time that the Kargil operation had almost started. It was not until many months later that I met Nawaz Sharif in Jeddah, where he was living after General Pervez Musharraf had banished him following the military coup in Pakistan. When I asked him about Kargil, he claimed that he did not know anything about the operation till Vajpayee informed him on the hotline about the intrusion. However, Musharraf said in a later interview that 'everybody was on board'.

I suspect Nawaz Sharif knew a bit about the operation just as General Ayub Khan knew about the infiltration which Zulfikar Ali Bhutto had arranged in 1965, leading to a war between India and Pakistan. Nawaz Sharif told me that he paid the price of trying to negotiate peace with India, something to which he said the military was opposed. This might well be true. For any kind of settlement on Kashmir the military would have to be involved, the Pakistanis say without hesitation. The military would not agree to any arrangement which meant the transfer of power from itself to civilian rulers.

Vajpayee, too, seemed to believe this. When I met him after the coup in Pakistan, he said, 'He (Nawaz Sharif) sacrificed himself for us.' Regarding the settlement on Kashmir, Vajpayee said, 'We were almost there.' He was referring to the behind-the-scene talks between R.K. Mishra, once a newspaperman and then a Vajpayee political advisor, and Niaz Naik, Pakistan's retired foreign secretary. I failed to scoop out what was the agreement which made Vajpayee make this statement. R.K. Mishra has remained silent on the matter. Niaz Naik has said in press interviews that there was a long way to cover for the settlement. What was the formula which the two countries had arrived at through Mishra and Niaz for Vajpayee to remark 'we were almost there', remains shrouded in secrecy.

17

Manmohan Singh

Manmohan Singh was the economic adviser to the government when I met him for the first time. Earlier I had seen him around in places like the India International Centre and Bhai Vir Singh Sahitya Sadan near Gole Market in Delhi, but had never talked to him. In our first conversation, he told me, 'You deserve the Bharat Ratna.' Those were the days when a gulf had developed between Hindus and Sikhs. I was a member of the Punjab Group which was talking to the Akalis on the one hand and the Government of India on the other to devise a formula which would allay Sikh fears.

Subsequently, when I was India's high commissioner in London, I had made efforts to bring the two communities closer. Manmohan Singh had heard and read about the extra mile I had travelled in London to reach the Sikh community.

My efforts were misunderstood by some fanatic Hindu groups and that had created problems for me back at home. Some MPs attacked me for being 'pro-Khalistan'. The then foreign minister, Inder Gujral, a personal friend, rang me up to inform me that some of my observations had irked the pro-Hindu lobby in Parliament and they criticized me for being 'pro-Sikh'.

When he met me at the Bhai Vir Singh Sahitya Sadan, Manmohan Singh remarked that he was 'proud' to be president of an organization where Kuldip Nayar was a member. However, the same Manmohan Singh did not invite me even for a cup of tea during his ten-year tenure as prime minister. I was a leading journalist and had headed more than one newspaper. Probably, he did not want to risk the annoyance of Sonia Gandhi who knew that I had relentlessly criticized her mother-in-law, Indira Gandhi. Much earlier, before he became prime minister and I was the Indian high commissioner in London, he had an urgent medical condition requiring heart bypass surgery. The London hospital where he eventually had his operation demanded a prior guarantee that his bills would be paid and I, as the high commissioner, offered to provide the necessary documents. As he himself commented at the time, 'Nobody knows me here.'

At the time Manmohan Singh was still not the economic adviser to the Indian government. He had the reputation, however, of being an eminent, Oxford-educated economist who had worked in the World Bank and had earned recognition.

He was reluctant to talk in Punjabi because he did not have the same command in it as he had in English. Manmohan Singh belonged to the lower middle class from Amritsar and had studied under street lights. At the Delhi School of Economics, he was a topper and created records which still remain unbeaten.

Prime Minister Narasimha Rao raised many eyebrows when he inducted Manmohan Singh as the finance minister in the cabinet. Manmohan Singh silenced his critics by his brilliance as an economist. His name is linked with the economic reforms of that time. He liberated the economy from the shackles of socialism and government control which Nehru had propagated. The public sector came tumbling down from the heights where Nehru had placed it. All are now agreed that India would have been among the top world economies if a person like Manmohan Singh had been there many years earlier. This is the common belief. The earlier comparatively modest growth of between four to five per cent instead of ten to twelve per cent, is due to the absence of a person like Manmohan Singh in the early years of Independence.

Like most English-educated persons, Manmohan Singh had no popular base. He was brought to the Rajya Sabha in 1991 from Assam where he had rented a house and even obtained a ration card so that he would be eligible for election from there. A ration card is needed by people who are marginalized. So the simple act of obtaining a humble ration card was not what one would expect of someone of Manmohan Singh's eminence. Yet he knew he could be elected from a constituency where Punjabis were in the majority. How ironic that he could not get the requisite support from Punjabis who otherwise supported his Congress party, when he contested for the Lok Sabha in 1999, from south Delhi.

Another irony is that the fact that Manmohan Singh had no popular base actually helped him in his political career. Congress President Sonia Gandhi selected him for the office of prime ministership because he had no power base and would depend on her. He was also her stalking horse.

For nearly ten years he remained as prime minister because he was a convenient front man for Sonia and her dynasty. Government files would go to Sonia Gandhi's house at 10 Janpath where Ahmed Patel, a bright Muslim leader, guided her in day-to-day government affairs. She had her own ideas of governance but they were not of the magnitude that India needed. Manmohan Singh was there as the prime minister to give them sanctity and authority. He was a nominee prime minister but he was adept in disposing of files, bureaucrat as he was for several years. Sonia Gandhi was particular to push him ahead of her on all public occasions. But it was quite a spectacle to watch on TV how unhappy he looked to occupy the chair ahead of Sonia Gandhi, his benefactor.

When he travelled abroad, it was his wife Gursharan who accompanied him. Between 2004 and 2014 he travelled to at least eighty foreign destinations ranging from Uzbekistan to Laos, the UK, the US, South Africa, China and the Maldives. Inevitably, it was his wife rather than Sonia who was by his side, so small wonder that he looked happier when abroad than in India.

When the BJP came to power the new prime minister, Narendra Modi, and his followers delighted in making fun of Manmohan Singh's perceived unblinding loyalty to Indira Gandhi and her dynasty. They mocked his integrity, saying he chose to ignore some of his party's most dubious deals. They even dug up the old story of how he got a ration card in Assam, saying he only acquired it to prove his residence and make himself eligible for election from that distant state. Whatever the facts about the ration card, none doubt Manmohan Singh's personal honesty. His strong point remains his humility.

18

Narendra Modi

I feel honoured that Prime Minister Narendra Modi has taken notice of my criticism. Indeed, he praised me and said: 'I respect veteran journalist Kuldip Nayarji; he fought for freedom during the Emergency—he may be a harsh critic of us but I salute him for this.' The prime minister and I are on the same page when it comes to the criticism of the Emergency which Indira Gandhi imposed in 1975.

We have never met face to face. But it is possible to evaluate him from his appearances on television and what he says in his speeches to the public. He has a superb grasp of Hindi and speaks extempore with the man and woman on the street. There is little doubt that he has a mass following.

Where we differ is in the shape of society we want. He belongs to the BJP, a political organ of the RSS, which wants to establish a Hindu Rashtra in the country, whereas I believe in a pluralistic society. His party divides people and I believe in what Mahatma Gandhi taught us about a multicultural nation where people of all religions can live together without fear.

I recall that Gandhi in his prayer meetings used to have recitations from the Quran along with the Gita and Bible. And if someone objected to this, he would not hold the meeting. The Mahatma's philosophy of pluralism was the nation's ethos. Prime Minister Modi respects Gandhi and says '*Sab ka saath, sab ka vikas.*' But his party's goal is to the contrary.

Modi disappoints many when he goes to Nagpur for exchanging views with the RSS high command. The Muslims are particularly peeved because they tend to see a society divided on the basis of religion, more so after the demolition of the Babri Masjid.

Happily, Modi has kept veteran BJP leaders like L.K. Advani and Murli Manohar Joshi at a distance from the affairs of the party and government. Modi's style of governance is also different from these leaders. But the direction in which he wants to take the nation is clear. A diluted form of Hindutva has spread throughout the country.

The prime minister has to ask himself whether this scenario is good for the people. A multicultural society like India has to stay pluralistic because that is what fits into the scheme of things. When key positions in education or other affairs of government are given to the trusted RSS men, the faith of liberals, the Muslims and others living on the peripheries, the minorities, is shaken. Modi has to give them confidence so that their contribution is considered equally important.

I find the minorities feeling insecure. They constitute one-fourth of the nation. The then Muslim League poisoned the minds of its community and created a situation where even drinking water was divided into two separate pitchers—Hindu pani/Muslim pani—one marked for the Hindus and the other for the Muslims at railways stations.

The Hindus were happy that the North-West Frontier Province, under the influence of Khan Abdul Ghaffar Khan, was with them. But otherwise, they did not give much leeway to the Muslims. The Congress had Maulana Abul Kalam Azad as one of its top leaders and he threw in his lot with the Hindus. Yet, the Muslim League did not move away from the path of division on the basis of religion.

Unfortunately, this affected the students who ate from different kitchens and preferred to form their own individual circles. In my final year at the Law College in Lahore, Qaid-e-Azam Mohammad Ali Jinnah had addressed the students. True, he emphasized that Hindus and Muslims were two nations but went on to exhort that they should stay together and develop the country. I expressed my doubt during the Q&A session and Jinnah assured us that India and Pakistan would be the best of friends.

Today, there is very little contact between the two. It is near impossible for Pakistanis to get a visa to come to India and for Indians to visit Pakistan. And my worst fears have come true. Many people on both sides believe that Kashmir is the impediment. I myself believe there is much truth in what Jawaharlal Nehru once said: 'Even if Kashmir were to be handed over to Pakistan on a platter, Pakistan would think of some other way to keep its quarrel with India alive, because Kashmir is only a symptom of a disease, and that disease is a hatred of India.'

Coming back to Prime Minister Modi, he appeared to have tried his best to foster relations with Pakistan soon after he took over. He even broke his journey at Lahore to convey his good wishes to then Prime Minister Nawaz Sharif while returning from Russia and Afghanistan. This was the first visit by an Indian prime minister in a decade. During their meeting, the two leaders had even discussed Kashmir.

In the last year of his term, Modi is not likely to take any initiative on Pakistan lest his government should start another debate, which may or may not help politically. His concentration is more likely to be on the non-Hindi-speaking states below the Vindhyas because the BJP looks quite strong in the Hindi-speaking states. The danger he faces is that the power is concentrated in him which means one-man rule.

Indira Gandhi was swept out of power when people found that she, too, had become a one-person governance. Unfortunately, there was no other tall leader to challenge her authority. Nor did she allow anybody to grow. The situation today is somewhat similar in the BJP. There is nobody to confront Modi. This is his strength as well as his weakness.

Whether the prime minister would be able to stitch loose ends together before the polls is anybody's guess. Modi is riding a horse which he cannot dismount before the elections. He would perforce have to depend on the RSS and its cadre to deliver the goods. Modi must be planning different strategies to fight the polls and it is clear that he will be the party's candidate for another term as prime minister from 2019.

It looks as if the other parties are going to come together and form some kind of a federal front. Their endeavour would be, as Congress leader Sonia Gandhi has said, to stop the return of Modi. At this juncture Modi would need his party the most. But how could that be possible when he himself has become the BJP?

Epilogue

A Note from the Family

The study had always been the heart of the house. Life revolved around this room. Cramped, a little chaotic, dominated by a rather cluttered desk, books, family photos and a lamp and a chair. Anyone who came—the door to the house was never locked—was ushered in here. Friend, family, foe, dissenter, this is where he would sit, gaze into the distance and have his conversation. Family weddings were planned in this room, heated exchanges over politics happened here, new in-laws met the family here, Wagah plans were discussed, scalding tea was drunk, samosas devoured and gossip exchanged. This is the room where he still lingers in his books and old typewriter by the window, his thoughts still on the bookshelves, a room that is the emptiest now.

Most importantly, this was where The Column was written. Each Wednesday—deadline day—he would sit at his desk to write, in a kurta, inevitably crumpled, with his clip board, the kind that children use for examinations, at hand. Newspapers would be piled around him. This routine is so deeply ingrained in the Nayar household—having been followed for over four decades—that Wednesdays instinctively feel different. His handwriting was an indecipherable scrawl in contrast to his thoughts which were always clear; his sentences precise. He never missed a deadline, even till the end, and he never forgot a conversation.

He passed away oddly enough on Wednesday—the day that loomed largest on his calendar. And a day that will now intrinsically be tied with him, in ours. It was here, sitting at the computer with Gopal and Mr Ramachandran to assist him, that he finished this book, just two weeks before he went to the hospital, never to come back. In the last few months, each time he spoke to any of the grandchildren, he would rattle off the number of words he had written. '5,000,' he told each grandchild excitedly. 'Only a few thousand more. Then, the book is over.' There was always one more he was working on. The next book was to be on Ballia, a flicker in the lamp of freedom. In 1942, after the Quit India movement, the telegraph lines were cut off in Ballia, and for a few blissful days, this town thought it was independent. Then, the British came back in full force to shatter the illusion. The brutality that ensued really shook him. Injustice kept him up nights.

On Leaders and Icons was to be the book for the great-grandchildren. He had three, all brand new. The dedication of each book was always discussed threadbare at family dinners. Like with everything, including the title of the book, everyone had a vote and every voice counted. It didn't matter how young you were, you were always taken seriously. He was a true democrat—a trait that no one else in the family seems to have inherited.

The last month, he worked on the book more or less fulltime. His friend Shyam Bhatia was in town and the two would sit at the computer, drinking endless cups of tea, tossing ideas back and forth, talking loudly in Punjabi and remembering all the people he had profiled. He took no notes. Yet, he remembered every conversation he had like it happened yesterday. What Shastri said to him, what he replied, the day Mahatma Gandhi died and how he crossed over at Wagah and how the people on both sides of the border were the same.

For a man who had lived through history—and watched India emerge from an idea to an independent nation—he was someone who always had hope. His desire to make a difference undiminished, and his optimism unscarred by cynicism. India would always be pluralistic, how could it not? If there was a battle to fight to make India better, even if it was a lost cause, or maybe just because it was, he would be the first one to stand up to fight. He never lost hope or his will to fight it. Till the end.

New Delhi   The Nayar Family
November 2018